299

HOW TO FIND GOD
in
Everyday Living

Adele Hooker

PublishAmerica

Baltimore

First printing

ISBN: 1-59129-413-4
PUBLISHED BY PUBLISHAMERICA BOOK
PUBLISHERS
www.publishamerica.com
Baltimore

Printed in the United States of America

Contents

Dedication

I'm pleased
to dedicate this book
to my daughter
Marydith
Who has had enough trials
to test God's promises
and prove them abundantly true.

In Gratitude

To my two dear and long-time-friends;
Susan Hamilton
for spending hours reading
and writing good suggestions
to make this book better.
And to
Vicki Cochran
for her much too complimentary
Foreword.
And to my dear husband,
Sam Hooker
for his help in
cooking and cleaning to
free me to be
glued to my computer
for the many, many hours it takes
to write one book and another
and another and another
etc., etc.

Meet Vicki Cockran

Before you read this "Foreword" I must tell you about Vicki. She has been a dear friend for many, many years. She is a Special Ed. teacher, for thirty-four years the wife of a very fine man, the mother of four wonderful children and a beautiful woman with a great heart of compassion. Because I trust her spiritual judgment, I asked her to read my manuscript. When she came back with such a positive response, I asked her to write the foreword. Now I feel inadequate to receive these complementary words.

And so I must say, all the wealth in this little volume was given me by the many sojourners who have gone on before. Some you will meet here. And I thank God most of all for my good friend and divine mentor, Jesus, (we wrote this together) and for the Holy Spirit who has been my constant guide in my quest for Abundant Living. Whatever good there is in this person that I am or this work you hold in your hands, all credit is theirs.

Foreword

How privileged you are to hold this book in your hands, for you are soon to be mentored by one of the finest teacher of this or any generation. As I read these pages I felt deep gratitude that as a young woman I sat at Adele Hooker's feet in a small group she called "Strugglers." I had never known anyone like her - so confident in God's word and the reality of his involvement in the lives of his children. She challenged me by her example of faith and practical Christian living. If God said it, she believed it and lived it! And what's more, she inspired us young ones in faith to find God just as real for ourselves.

As I read this book in its rough draft form, I recalled many of the stories and teachings for they changed my life. You will love reading them, too! I know you'll want to read this book from cover to cover without stopping, for it will capture your heart and mind. But then go back and take time with each chapter to prayerfully apply and learn its truths. The teachings are practical for anyone who's serious about an exciting life that pleases God and blesses others. God has much to teach us through his dear servant Adele Hooker, who has found God to be vital and real in everyday living.

Vicki Cochran

INTRODUCTION

This book is intended for those who want more out of life; those who want to know the peace and joy of having God in their everyday living and for those who want to know how to make sense out of seemingly senseless happenings. Our Heavenly Father sent his son to walk this earth-life with us, and to guide us to that Life Abundant which comes from the heart of God.

It's a delight for me to attempt to share the beauty and yes, even splendor and glory, that I have been privileged to know as I yielded my life fully to my beloved Lord. I have delighted and still delight in learning his will and his ways. I even welcome the struggle it takes to conform my life to his will.

Oh how precious Jesus has become and how beloved is his Holy Spirit as they have been my teachers and guides for these fifty-four years since I first made that absolute surrender to God which for so long I foolishly feared to make.

If this little book helps others to find the path of Abundant Living in their everyday life then all the moments I have been glued to this computer are repaid. For they, too, will joy here on their earth-path and I shall joy with them in heaven.

JESUS SAYS COME

Dear Child,
Does your load seem too heavy?
I have come to share it with you.
Are your hurts too deep for salving?
I am your healer.
Do you know how to tap into
my loving grace?
Read my Word.
I have guided my servants
to bring you instruction.
Does the world seem too confusing?
Come to me in prayer.
Please know,
your earth life is a schooling.
Teachers, helpers
have been sent to you.

And I have come to walk with you.
I have come to bring you
the wisdom, the power, and the glory
of your Father God.

Give me your open heart
and you will have my Presence
to strengthen and to bless you
with the peace and the joy
found in God alone.
Have you been chewing
on the dry crusts
of this world?
Come, child, and partake.
There is milk and honey
in the Kingdom of God.
Come.
I am with you.
I will guide you.
Come.

AH

CHAPTER 1
MERCIES OF THE LORD

Are you eager to find a way to live more abundantly? Jesus gives us a simple formula for it.

He says, "If you will live in me and let me live in you, you will find life in abundance. My life is fulfillment and in it is found love, joy, and peace." (John 15)

After many years of working this formula I have found Jesus' words to be true. When we turn our attention to him and let him guide our lives everything has meaning and value. He does not remove all the hills and valleys from our path. He does not make everything smooth and easy. But he guides us to live in wiser ways and he leads us in more productive paths. The scorching things he uses to refine us as pure gold is refined by fire. And we will see, he makes all things turn to our good.

If we will allow ourselves to be instructed by Jesus, difficulties will bless us. Because of them we grow wiser, stronger and nearer to God, who is the source of our health and strength. When we remove challenges from our children and give them only what they want, we foil God's plan for their lives. In the same way we foil God's plan for our own Abundant Living when we shun the hard places or muddle through them without God's guidance.

Somehow we have come to believe life was designed to be smooth, always. Reality tells us differently. It takes deep cuts to fashion jewels from raw stones. Shaping and faceting diamonds demands grinding and polishing. It takes friction to create a gem. God's desire for us is that we become as precious gems in spiritual character.

Hard times come in all our lives. And bad things happen to good people. But God does not leave us to suffer them alone or for no purpose. He wants to guide us, to strengthen and encourage us. If we will draw near to him he will comfort us, even as he shapes and polishes.

Let me share a bitter experience with you and tell you how near and dear Jesus was to me and my family through it all.

It was 9:30 on Friday night, September 3, 1999, when I heard my daughter's anguished wail over the telephone, "Mama, Joshua was killed in an accident. I can't stand it! I can't stand it! Can you come?"

"Yes, Honey, I'll come right away," I reassured her.

That was the beginning of a nightmare we wanted to awaken from…but couldn't.

Joshua was driving a BMW at the time of the accident. The car he hit head-on was a Ford Explorer which contained a couple and their three children. A young couple on vacation was in a third vehicle, a sedan, which was pulling a travel trailer. The sedan crashed into the Explorer, leaving tire marks that arched across the side of the Explorer. All the cars were totaled, but the other passengers had only the slightest injuries.

Joshua, our twenty-five-year-old darling, tall, handsome, big-warm-hugger, full of humor, how could he be taken from us? How could we live without him? And God knows, it was too much!

Marydith already lost a son. Eric drowned when he was twenty-two months old. His father drowned ten years later. Joshua had been in an accident a week earlier that required twenty-six stitches in his back and totaled a car. Now he was dead. To add to her woes, for several years Marydith has been suffering from Chronic Fatigue Syndrome. How much more should one person take? How much more did God require of her?

And the questioning thoughts continued, What had we done, as parents and grandparents, to deserve all these catastrophes? We strove to be faithful servants, as Marydith did. We loved God. We trusted him with all we had.

I hurried to put a few things in an overnight bag and within ten minutes I was on my way. It would take three hours to get from our home in Portland, Oregon to Sisters, Oregon where Marydith lives. All the way over the mountains, for the full three hours, a refrain was repeated near my left ear. It said, "I will sing of the mercies of the Lord forever, I will sing, I will sing." I didn't pay any attention to it. It surely didn't come from my own thinking. At that time I was in no mood to sing and I couldn't see a mercy of the Lord in this dreadful tragedy.

When Nick, another of my grandsons who was driving for me, and I arrived at my daughter's home she was sitting on the sofa in utter grief. Crushed by sorrow, she cried, "It's too much, Mama. It's too much. I can't bear it. It's too much!"

"Darling," I said, beating back my own need to wail, "Yes, it's too much. But God's grace is sufficient. He said it would be. Either it is or it isn't. If it isn't then we can't trust him. But I'm a believer. I believe. There is a mercy in God for us and 'balm in Gilliad' for our wounded souls." The refrain was still singing at my left ear, "I will sing of the mercies of the Lord forever. I will sing. I will sing." However, I still didn't feel it was coming from within me.

We sat up all night and wept and moaned and hugged and hoped for comfort. But no comfort comes from words. There are no words in the human language for grief such as this.

The next day Marydith said, "I need to tell my good friend, Camille, about Joshua. She loved him so much, and I don't want her to hear it from someone else. I need to go to the river where she's gone for the Labor Day week-end." I said, "Go. I'll stay here and wait for the others who are coming."

While I was alone, I sat in an old fashioned rocking chair thinking and praying. I said, "Jesus, I know you are here right beside me. You said you would be and I believe you. Please talk to me."

This gentle voice came quietly into my left ear, "I've been singing to you all night. You will see the mercy of the Lord even in this. And you will sing. In time, Marydith will sing. She will sing, sing, sing."

"How can that be?" I asked.

Then He proceeded to show me his mercies as I sat, listening.

I thought about the young family. How would I feel if the mother, father or the children had died in the accident? Or if the young couple were dead?

Small comfort in the face of the grief we were bearing?

Oh No! A big mercy!

How would we feel if Josh had survived with head injuries that caused abnormal brain function? Or that put him in a wheel chair for life? Would we choose that?

No! Oh No!

A mercy? Yes, yes indeed.

I thought, "Lord, you saved everyone else. Why not Joshua?"

"This was Joshua's time to go to another place to work and to serve." These were the words I heard in my mind.

Then I felt a strong sense of Joshua's presence in the room, so I asked, "Joshua, do you have to go some place?"

I heard my grandson's voice say, "Yes. But I'm going later. I'm going to hang around these guys for awhile."

I sensed Jesus had given him the privilege to stay and comfort us: his mother, brother, grandparents, and all his other relatives and friends for whom he cared so much.

Quietly I thanked God for the mercies he had just revealed to me. Although I was not relieved of my pain, I knew "there is a balm in Gillead" and there is a comforting Savior who walks with us and talks with us. He said, "My sheep know my voice."

As the song writer said, "I have walked alone with Jesus in a fellowship divine... I have seen him. I have known him. And he deigns to walk with me. And the glory of his presence shall be mine eternally ."

Was I comforted that day sitting in Marydith's house?

By faith, I could say through my tears, "God is good. His mercies endure forever. And yes, I believe. In time we will sing again. We will sing."

My experience of talking with Joshua may not seem credible to many believers. There was a time when I would have questioned someone who claimed to have had conversation with a deceased relative. However, in the past fifty years I've known of many others. These were Christians who told me that their deceased loved ones had come to them with comforting words.

And besides, I've finally reckoned with the fact that Jesus has the right and the power to do whatever he chooses, regardless of my dogmatic beliefs.

That was no little concession for me to make.

It was less than a year after Marydith's great loss that God did give her a song. She called me one day and said, "Mama, I have two grandbabies. Last night Jill and Brett got identical twin boys and I was able to be there for the birthing."

Jesus said Marydith would sing, sing, sing! Although she still weeps, she also sings.

CHAPTER 2
JESUS PEOPLE ARE PEACEFUL

Have you found the secret for survival in times of deepest distress? Have you found your way in the darkest night to the comforting arms of your Heavenly Father?

Jesus came in a physical body to show us the way.

He gave us his Word to instruct us, a map to mark out the road, and his Holy Spirit to be our guide and our teacher. He has also given us godly people and yes, angels too, to draw near to assist us with our needs. He has given us the great gift of prayer. How can we resist this giving, caring Father? How can we go day after day and not take time to commune with him in prayer?

Down this road, rough and winding, Jesus has committed himself to be our traveling companion. He both knows the way and will help carry the load. Life can become burdensome, painful, wearisome and toilsome. But in our walk with Jesus we can come to know peace and joy even through the hardest times and the roughest places.

I was impressed with a small incident my husband, Sam, told me about. He had come home from the dry cleaners with a suit that he had cleaned. He said a young Asian woman checked his suit in earlier in the week and when he went back for it that day she talked to him. "You look so peaceful," she said several times. With that, Sam told her he was a minister. She said, "Since I come to this country I find Jesus people are peaceful. I pray to Jesus every morning. Jesus people are peaceful." She said it again and again.

That too, has been my experience. Since I've linked up with Jesus, that is, linked up with him in a personal way, I have been given a deep peace beyond my understanding, and that even in my most sorrowing times.

The song writer says, "There is a place of quiet rest near to the heart of God." Jesus led me to that place of peace. He'll lead you there, too, if you will take time each day to draw near to the heart of God.

The Asian woman was right, "Jesus' people are peaceful."

CHAPTER 3
A MAP AND A GUIDE

The book of John begins with these words, "In the beginning was the Word and the Word was with God and the Word was God…And the Word was made flesh and dwelt among us."

That Word is Jesus. God has given us both a written and a Living Word. The wisdom of God is in both. If we would have wise counsel through life we need to study the written word and live with the Living Word.

When traveling to an unfamiliar destination, it is only common sense to study a map. If it's a trip in a foreign country it's important to get instructions from a knowledgeable person as well. None of us have lived this life before. It is a foreign land. Yet multitudes ignore the Bible, that marvelous map which God has given us for this life's journey.

When Sam and I traveled in Africa I realized how utterly lost we'd be if we had not had a guide to lead us. That is not unlike life's journey. There are many pitfalls on the way and many evils that would waylay us.

On our way to Africa we stopped in Switzerland to sightsee. While waiting for the train from Geneva to Lucerne we visited with a couple who were also waiting. When we told them we were en route to Africa the man said, "We've just come back from our safari and we should warn you. Be careful. Don't be deceived by the beautiful animals that look so peaceful. A family that was traveling in their car at the time we were had a horrible accident. They stopped to take pictures of some lions lying not far from the road. The father got out of the car to get a better picture. And just that swiftly the lion attacked and killed him. He was torn to pieces right there before his little family. The animals may not look dangerous, but they are."

The Bible tells us Satan is like a roaring lion seeking whom he may devour. (I Peter 5:8)

Satan and his many imps and henchmen may look as benign as a sleeping lion but they are as treacherous and more so.

I surely would not want to travel through Africa without a guide. Just as surely, I would not want to travel through this "foreign country" of life without a guide. Multitudes have tried it and multitudes are still doing so. Sooner or later most get torn and mutilated by the enemy of their souls. Many young people have paid with their lives for drugs and alcohol and other evils Satan has used to tempt them.

Even when traveling in safer places than the jungles of Africa, it doesn't make sense to journey without assistance.

One year we traveled throughout the Holy Lands with a group of people. The streets were marked in Jerusalem and we had a map. But without our wonderful guide we would not have known the names of the interesting sights nor how to get to them. Our guide was knowledgeable, caring and a great comfort when we had other particular needs.

I often grieve for people who do not have Jesus. They miss a world of wonder and beauty. Not all these things are in tangible form. I've found that the greatest joys are spiritual.

The Bible is our map and our Christian friends are fellow travelers. But still we need the intimacy of Jesus, the Lord of

Life, to walk with us and to instruct us in our many unique situations. He knows the path we walk and he knows the scenic routes we are privileged to take. He wants to guide and instruct us so that we can live wisely and abundantly.

Have you gone to school with a student who was rebellious and refused to listen or to do any work?

I taught English (now called "Language Arts") in public high school. Some students refused to study and spent most of the class time trying to disrupt it. There is that kind of people in the school of life, too. This book is not for them nor would they be reading it. But for you who want to learn, to step up into a higher mode of living, to get more out of life, this book will help you. But more important, give time to study the map, The Greatest Book Ever Written, The Bible. Take time to develop an intimate relationship with it's author, The Greatest Guide And Companion You Could Ever Find, Jesus.

CHAPTER 4
HONEY OUT OF A ROCK?

Jesus came to give us abundant life. He is eager to help us attain it. If you take time to walk with him, to study and observe, and put into practice what you learn, you will be amazed at the peace, love and joy you will receive. You will have a loving teacher and companion beyond your wildest dreams.

But this is not a quick fix. It is newness of life. It is life begun in a new way. Living takes time.

When a new cause comes into a life new effects occur.

When you sincerely open your heart and ask Jesus to come in and live with and in you, he is the new cause that brings new effects. Some of those new effects are peace and joy. They may come quickly. On the other hand, they may emerge slowly. We are all unique with our individual differences. But when Jesus, the Prince of Peace, comes, peace will inevitably come with him.

The Bible says every hair on your head is numbered. God knows us that individually. Maybe you have thought of God as being far off in heaven some place. Not so. He is EVERYWHERE. He is NEAR. He is more personal, more intimate than the air you breathe. He is with you and he wants to live in you with loving response.

He is your Heavenly Father. He created you. He loves you. He wills only good for you. He is wisdom personified. And with this love and wisdom he will live in you. He will do for you not only what is good for you, but what is best. He will cause everything that happens to do you good and to bless you.

There will be times you will feel discouraged. You will think God doesn't care or that he is not near. Some things will cause you to mistakenly feel disappointed in him, thinking he allowed a bad thing to happen to you. Yes, at the moment it may seem bad. However, in time you will understand his wisdom and see how much you needed that experience in order to go through future ones successfully. Early in our ministry I had such an experience which I thought was horrible. I'll tell you about it.

When my husband, Sam, and I were first in the ministry we were badly hurt, especially by a couple I'll introduce to you later. The hurt seemed so bad I felt I could not forgive them. The more I thought about what they did to us the greater was my anger until I realized I hated them. I knew I couldn't be an honest pastor's wife and teach love when I hated. I'm an honest person at heart and I couldn't live a hypocritical life. I prayed about it but my prayers seem to be of no avail. I considered how I could get out of the ministry without destroying Sam's call. It troubled me greatly. Finally, I sought God more desperately than I had ever sought him in my life before. And I came to a wonderful peace through an intimate relationship with Jesus that I did not know existed for me. (I'll tell you about this in more detail later.)

For all these years I have enjoyed the delicious peace I found in that experience. Later I learned how very important it was for God to allow me to suffer so. I found every iota of the schooling I got from that bitter experience to be of great value.

If you walk with Jesus, God will not allow any day or any

experience of your life to be wasted. Each day, if you put your trust solidly in him, every single thing that happens to you will bear its own good fruit.

Oh how good he is to those who trust him! He brings sweetness out of the hardest places.

"Honey in a rock?"

Oh yes!

CHAPTER 5
NEW CAUSE = NEW EFFECTS

A wise man said, "If you understand God, it is not God. For he is then too small to be God."

God is beyond our reasoning. We cannot understand his ways. They are beyond our wisdom.

He is creator and creative.

He asks us to have faith in him. Faith is believing God will produce what he promises. Our faith is proven by our actions. If we have faith then we will trust and we will obey. When he says "Abide in me," we need to respond by saying, "Yes, Lord, I will abide in you." We "abide" by giving Jesus thought, time and attention.

If you really want more out of life than you are now getting, consider Jesus' instructions. Act on them. Be consistent and persistent. Cause and effect is still a universal, unbreakable, unfailing law. Enter a new cause into your life and you will gain a new effect!

Jesus is the "New Cause" that came into my life and a Grand New Effect came with him. At that time I needed someone to share spiritually with me. I was desperate. But I had no person I could go to. God in his goodness sent me spiritual guidance in books and other writings. I learned from those Christian writers who had walked the path before me.

The first step on this path to Abundant Life is to accept Jesus as your daily, intimate companion. Even if you asked Jesus to come into your life earlier, you can do so again with the intent to make it a more deeply committed agreement.

One day an older woman asked my husband, Sam, to come see her. When he got there she said, "I want to renew my vows with Jesus. I've neglected him and our relationship. I want to renew my commitment to him." Sam prayed with her as she asked Jesus to forgive her for neglecting him. Then she and Sam held hands and repeated the twenty-third Psalm together. She gained the inner peace which she longed for.

When we commit our lives to Jesus we have a marriage relationship with him. He takes first place in our lives. We commit to him our love, our time and our attention.

Jesus is always near. He waits for us to ask him into our lives anew. Here is a prayer you can use to commit yourself to him.

Dear Lord Jesus,

I'm tired of going my way. I want to go a better way. Will you please help me? I'm willing to go your way. Where I have done wrong, been unkind or rebellious, please forgive me. Help me to do the right things that bring the right results in my life.

Please guide me.

Help me to be willing to follow you. Help me take time to learn from you and your Word, the Bible.

I'd appreciate it if you'd relieve my troubled mind and bring me peace. You know my problems. You know my needs. And you know my deepest desires. Please help me to believe you care and are looking out for my best interests. And please help me to have patience and endurance as I learn to walk with you.

Thank You for all you will do for me. Please give me strength to do my part.

Amen.

Prayer is more than talking at God. It is talking to God from your heart, being genuine, and then listening for his reply.

Although it is not always easy to harness our attention and hold it on Jesus, prayer is really a simple thing to do. The Holy Spirit is able to help us learn to pray effectively. But he waits for us to invite him to do so.

Ask him to help you. And be aware. He will.

CHAPTER 6
TRADING COPPER FOR GOLD

The Bible says, "As a man thinketh in his heart, so is he." That which we think, we will become. In E. Stanley Jones' book entitled *Abundant Living*, he says, "What gets your attention gets you." If you want Jesus to help you find abundant life, you must give him your attention. We are so accustomed to filling all our time looking after our own and others' needs and desires that setting time to learn from Jesus and nurturing our own souls is foreign to most of us.

Old habits aren't easy to break. It will take time, effort and consistency to establish new patterns. But you must establish new patterns if you want new results.

The prophet called out to the people, "Choose you this day whom you will serve." The voice of God still goes out with the same cry, "CHOOSE YOU THIS DAY WHOM YOU WILL SERVE." That call comes to us individually. It comes to you, it comes to me - personally.

Jesus said, "I am the vine. You are the branches. If you will live in me, I will live in you." His energy, his spirit, will flow through you and give you life abundant and "your joy will be full." (John 15:1-11) This is a call for relationship. Relationship calls for commitment. Tell Jesus you will spend special time each day learning to know him and learning from him. Ask him to help you keep that commitment.

Set a time and a place where you can give your full attention to your relationship with Jesus. Choose a time and place when you will not be distracted by family, telephone or TV. Start with ten minutes.

You have twenty four hours in a day. That's one thousand, four hundred and forty minutes every day. If you can't carve a little ten or fifteen minute space out of that big block of over a thousand minutes of time, you should reassess your values. Do you want to upgrade your life?

When I started spending time with Jesus, I tried everything else but getting up before the family. Finally, I realized if I really wanted to have a consistent private time to spend moments with Jesus, I had to surrender a lesser experience for a greater one. I had to give up some of my own personal time in sleep.

I set the morning alarm fifteen minutes earlier and forced - I mean forced!—myself to get out of a warm bed into a cold room. I discovered how strong the physical desires are compared to the spiritual. It seemed like a great big sacrifice. But in time I realized the wonderful benefit. I increased the minutes to thirty and then to an hour.

I had some hassles to overcome. The main one was my husband's unwillingness to let me disturb his sleep with the alarm ringing early. When I asked the Lord to awaken me, he did. Then Sam complained that he didn't sleep after I got up.

Sam's a good person. He didn't understand why I couldn't find a time during the day when it would not disturb him.

Well, I couldn't find a different time so I just had to accept the hassle and do what I felt was right for myself. I persisted against all odds.

If you will persist, I think you will be amazed how Jesus will be right there to help you. But you have to exercise your will and your faith.

Remember Jesus said, "Whatsoever you desire when you pray, believe and you'll receive it." (Mark 11:24) Believing means acting to attaining it. We are workers together with God, the Bible says. He will not be cheated in a covenant. If we won't work on our commitment to him we need not expect him to work for us either.

Ask Jesus to help you trade a lesser good for a greater one; copper for gold.

Sound good?

Believe me, it is!!

CHAPTER 7
BLESSED ARE THE HUNGRY

Some people find evenings before going to bed works better for their quiet time. Ask Jesus to guide you to the most effective time and to help you get started. Ask him to help you to become spiritually hungry so you will feel your deep need of these times with him.

In Jesus' wonderful Sermon On The Mount (Matthew 5) he says "Blessed are they which do hunger and thirst after righteousness." Jesus, himself is our righteousness. We have none of our own. Jesus is glad to help us hunger and thirst after him.

It's a sign of ill health not to get physically hungry. That holds true spiritually as well. If we feel we need to eat physically three times a day with snacks in between, what makes us think we can be healthy spiritually without daily rations?

You ask, "What to eat?" The Word!

John 1:1 says, "In the beginning was the Word and the Word was with God and the Word was God...and the Word became flesh and dwelt among us...(v14)" Jesus is the Living Word. The Bible is the written Word. The Sermon On the Mount is both living and written. If you read it slowly and digest it, it will bring life, health and strength to you. Memorize Jesus' words. Read them over and over again until they become a part of you. This is the way you digest your spiritual food. Just as physical food becomes flesh and blood to your body, so this spiritual food becomes flesh and blood to your spiritual body, your soul. It becomes Life.

It's "Christ in you the hope of glory." (Col. 1:27) The more you take in of him the more his radiant energy will shine in you.

As the sun gives light, life and health to the physical body, so the Son of God gives Light, Life and Health to your spiritual body.

Once we make the commitment to become a healthy person both physically and spiritually we are well on our way down this path to abundant living!

If you aren't accustomed to reading the Bible it is helpful to start with Jesus' Sermon On The Mount in Matthew 5:1-10. Spend time with it. Don't hurry through. Ask Jesus to reveal the deeper meanings in each verse. In this way you "eat" the Word, the "Bread of Life."

Feel the blessing of God beaming on you. Does it provide the emotional warmth you desire? Does it give you the love you have been craving? This blessedness is an appropriate dose of whatever you need. Feel it coming to you as you read the Word.

After you have thoroughly "eaten" Jesus' sermon, you might ask him where you should go next in the Bible. Or you might go back and start at the beginning of the New Testament. However, it's okay to skip the names of Jesus' ancestors and begin with Matthew 1:18. Matthew, Mark, Luke and John will get you acquainted with Jesus' life and miracles. Jesus himself will meet you in the quiet of your mind and heart. He will teach you about his will for you. Listen for his still, small voice. He always speaks in love. You will come to recognize it. By this he imparts his love and grace, the source of his Abundance in Living.

We hear with our ears, but it is our mind which registers what our ears take in. In this way our mind takes in the ideas of other people. Why not let Jesus place his thoughts and attitudes in your mind? It was a wonderful thing for me when I found out Jesus wanted to share my mind, too. I get his thoughts in my mind and so we share together. I agree with the song writer who said, "And he walks with me and he talks with me and he tells me I am his own. And the joys we share as we tarry there, none other has ever known." ("In The Garden" by C. Austin Miles)

In time you will come to experience these floods of joy as you talk with and listen to Jesus in the quiet of your mind and heart. He loves you. You will come to know it when you spend time developing this intimate relationship with him.

CHAPTER 8
TASTE AND SEE

The gospel of John is my favorite book of The Bible and chapter 15:1-11 are my favorite verses. It was an exciting discovery when I found I could live in Jesus and he would live in me. It's still the most exciting thing in my life. Just thinking of it and talking about it makes me want to shout, "Hallelujah! Praise you God for your most wonderful gift, Jesus, my precious Lord!"

To think Jesus, the very Son of God, would come to us personally, live inside our minds and hearts, and give us his Spirit is unfathomable!

I would never expect the queen of England or even our president to visit me, let alone live with me. Yet God's own son has condescended to do so! Sometimes I think if that doesn't thrill a person's heart that person must not have a heart. The Bible says we are dull of hearing and dull of understanding.

How well we've proven that!

Satan is in the business of blinding people. He tells us "what is good is bad" and "what is bad is good." Sadly, too many people believe him. How true, we have to "taste and see that the Lord is good." (Ps. 34:8)

I know Jesus wants to bless my day. Often in my morning

quiet time I ask him to direct me to what he wants me to read for that day. Then I open my Bible at random and read whatever my eyes fall on. Usually it meets the particular need I have and I know Jesus directed me to it. I suggest you try this approach sometime. Watch God lead you to the specific scriptures that meet your need. It is one of the many sweet things you will find in your "Quiet Time." But there are so many others. You will find them for yourself and you'll know Jesus was right there with you, guiding you. But be patient. Just keep in mind that a weed will grow quickly in your garden but it takes time to grow a tomato plant, a beautiful flower or a handsome tree.

I find the writings of other spiritual persons strengthening, too. Wherever we find the inspiration of Christ, there is meat and bread, wine and honey for our souls.

In the rich little book *Madam Guyon,* by Jan Johnson, Madam Guyon tells what this quiet inner prayer meant to her. She says, "I noticed how this prayer of the heart gave me stronger faith. I was fearful and intimidated before but now feared nothing. I felt confidence in God, wanting to do His will."

And, "The Beloved himself attracted my heart. Pleasures that others loved appeared dull to me; I wondered how I could ever have enjoyed them." (Ch. 3 p. 26)

Fully I agree with Madam Guyon! The sweetest times of my life are when I am communing with Jesus or doing something for or with him. For instance, writing this book is a joy because I sense so keenly we are doing it together.

Sometimes the writings of other Christians speak as loudly to one's soul as Bible passages. Another love of mine is *Guideposts* Magazine. Its stories are brief and soul enriching. *Angels on Earth*, published by Guideposts, is also a joy to me. You'll find God has dozens of ways to bless you when you start recognizing them.

It's important to become aware of his blessings. The more you read of them and experience them, the greater your everyday living will be enriched.

CHAPTER 9
SWEET CONVERSATION

To begin with, prayer is simply talking to Jesus and listening to hear him talk to you. He talks to you through the words you read. But he also talks to you in that "still, small voice" within your mind. If you aren't listening, you won't hear him. I urge you to listen so the Spirit of God can speak to you.

I like what Sam teasingly said to a man one day. Sam misquoted the scripture a bit to say, "And I will walk behind you and you will hear my voice." (Lev. 26:12)

The man quipped in a disgruntled tone, "I don't hear him talk to me!"

Sam responded, "Well, God don't waste his breath on people who won't listen. If you wanna hear him ya gotta listen!"

I readily confess, hearing God's voice takes practice as surely as a babe needs practice to hear his mother's voice and understand her words.

In prayer, it's also of great benefit to acknowledge the tremendous marvel, the wonder, and the glorious power of God in all his creation. At first you may not feel this power. But as you affirm it you will begin to recognize it, and after a while, feelings of joy and wonder and glory will come. Look around you. See the good things God has created. Acknowledge the good in your life. Praise God!

You may think, there isn't much good in my life. Again, what gets your attention gets you. Turn your attention from the negatives to the positives.

For the moment, you may not see any positives in your life.

At one time, I had built such a mountain of negatives that I couldn't look over it to see any positives.

Jesus saved me from my negative, angry and self-pitying thinking and feelings. To be saved from my self-centered addiction was a great miracle. Only God could have done it for me. I have praised him for it for over fifty years. I shall ever praise him for so great a gift: the freedom to be positive, appreciative, hopeful, and grateful.

He gave me freedom from that self-centered life. Now I continue to pray, "Lord, save me from myself."

In William Glasser's course, "Reality Therapy," which trains workers to help drug-addicted people, I was told when a person didn't feel like doing the right thing to have them "fake it until you feel it." This applies to prayer, too. It is a choice of the will. If you don't feel like praising God, "Fake it 'till you feel it." Soon you will feel it. And in time it will be genuine.

CHAPTER 10
IMAGINE! IMAGINE! IMAGINE!

Look around you. See a tree, a flower, the sun, moon, stars or anything of God's creation. Acknowledge his marvelous creative work. Tell him you praise him for his wonderful creative power. And tell him you are giving yourself to him to create a new life within you. Thank him by faith that that new life is starting to grow!

Jesus is the Tree Of Life. Envision yourself a branch on that tree. See your branch beginning to bud and put out new shoots. This Tree Of Life bears the abundance of fruit called, love, joy, peace, goodness, mercy, kindness, generosity. All these pleasant fruits and more will grow on your branch when it is embedded in Christ Jesus, The Tree of Life.

Keep envisioning your life like a branch growing out of that tree. Inspect your branch often. Ask Jesus to help you recognize your need. Admit to the bitter fruit you don't want. Don't try to hide it or deny it. Tell Jesus about it. And ask him to help you prune off what he doesn't want growing there.

Each day thank him that his energy is flowing through your branch to develop the particular fruits you want. Whether it's peace, joy, love, kindness or another positive virtue, envision that fruit growing healthy on your branch.

As I've told you before, the most exciting scripture I ever encountered is the first part of John 15 that tells us Jesus will live in us and we can live in him. And if we stay attached, he will prune us and his energy will flow through us to bear an abundance of fruit. And our joy will be full. I keep reading that and I keep surrendering to the good gardener. I want my branch to be full and abundant with every good fruit.

A little scheme I devised for myself early on was to take one fruit for a week, such as patience or kindness. I imagined it budding and growing into all its fullness. Whenever I thought of it during the day I'd see myself nurturing it by giving it good thoughts and whatever good actions I could at the time. The next week I'd add another fruit to my determination to be abundantly fruitful.

If you really want abundant life you have to grow an abundant crop of beautiful, positive attitudes. These are the fruits. See if you can adopt this plan or a variation of it. Fit it into your schedule and your way of living. Give your attention to pursue it. I promise you, you will find yourself growing in the many graces of Christ. And you will have more fun than you can imagine.

The key is to imagine the fruit you want, imagine it growing on your branch (your inner self) and imagine Your branch (your mind and heart) firmly embedded in the vine from which the nurturing substance comes, Christ Jesus.

In Sacramento, California Sam and I visited a grape grower. I was amazed at the huge bunches of gigantic grapes the farmer had hanging on these vines. I said, "I've never seen grapes like this. One grape is almost as big as my thumb. How do you do it?"

He showed me as he said, "We prune the vines severely. Then when they're growing and putting on new shoots, we go through the vineyard again and prune more branches off the same vines. That leaves fewer grapes but much bigger ones. Of course we have to see that the soil is right. And the weather has to cooperate, but the pruning is very important."

After we left and we were driving away I meditated on the farmer's grapes and what he told me about raising these big, luscious fruits. "Okay," I said to God, "I see, if you're a good gardener, as the Bible says you are, then you have no choice but to prune me. And I want to raise a good crop in my spiritual life. So I give you permission to prune me in any way and as much as you see I need. I loath to think I might be a spindly, weak branch that bears scrubby fruit. And so I make this commitment to you. Even when I fret and moan at your pruning, don't listen to me. Go ahead and prune."

Through the years God has shown me many things he wanted to prune from my life. At times I've shivered with fright. But I've never, by the grace of God, said, "Stop! Don't prune any farther."

For example, one of the negative traits which I think looks ugly in a person is stinginess. There was a time I was walking through my garden (my inner self) with God, the gardener. We were examining my fruit. For the first time I saw clearly, in myself, this distorted trait. My stinginess was like a vine growing scrubby grapes. I saw a poverty complex. It could have been fostered by the fact that I grew up during the deep depression. How it came didn't matter. It was there. I saw it. And I knew it didn't look any better on me than it did on others. I asked Jesus to cleanse me of this ugly thing. "Please Jesus, prune stinginess from my branch," I prayed. Then I ask him to help me grow the plump fruit of generosity so that he and I could both enjoy a healthy, beautiful branch on his vine. Now I keep working to have healthy grapes on that branch. And believe me, it's fun, fun, fun! to be prayerfully and carefully giving and helping others.

Stinginess comes in many forms; time withheld from those we love or could help, a little note of encouragement unwritten, even an encouraging word or compliment withheld when the occasion called for it, grumbling when a family member needs to buy something. Here are some good antidotes; gifts given when nobody expects them, a compliment for no apparent reason, a drop-in visit for a few minutes just out of the blue, and, of course, our tithe released to God with a grateful heart.

Another trait I have asked God to prune from my branch is talking badly about another person. I can't think of any more withered, moldy fruit in a Christian's life than that. Now when I see it, it seems so rotten I can almost smell it. There was a time I didn't see it in its reality and I joined in with others. The clearest way I was made to see slander or gossip was the experience I had with an otherwise lovely person who relished the superior feeling she got from this dreadful act. At that time I was the target of her active gossip. God showed her that it was the devil's territory. Long before this I had my own struggle with it. But I didn't realize until then how Satan enjoyed dragging God's children onto his foul playground.

So - as you imagine your branch, ask God to show you what he wants to prune away. Then imagine the good fruit you want to grow. Call it by name; joy, peace, gentleness, generosity. See it growing on your branch. Imagine! Imagine! Imagine! And you'll be surprised to see how inspired you'll be to grow your bumper crop. Imagination is a very valuable and abundantly productive gift. God has given it bountifully to mankind. Surely he is pleased to see us using it for our spiritual growth. So Imagine! Imagine! Imagine!

You'll be richer in all ways for it.

CHAPTER 11
JOY IN FORGIVENESS

If you have never repented of your sin, do so now. Jesus'blood washes us white as snow. Surrender your past so you can have a new beginning. Ask Jesus to separate you from your sinful past. You will be amazed at the joy there is in forgiveness.

If you don't think you have sinned, you should know the Bible says, "All have sinned and come short of the glory of God." Your sin may be self-righteousness, pride or maybe both. But chances are it's rebellion against God and his ways. Perhaps your sin is fear of God. Are you fearful God will ask you to do or to give what you think you cannot do or give? (or what you don't want to?)

Earlier I struggled with that fear because I didn't trust God to be a good and loving Heavenly Father. My unwillingness to give myself completely to God was a sin. Sin means "missing the mark." Whenever we live selfishly we miss the mark of the high calling Jesus has for us.

Here is a paragraph taken from the Oncology Class Paper (page 13) written by Doctor Margo Abshier in 1994. The title is, "Faith: How To Activate Faith To Receive A Miracle."

....It is important to ask God's forgiveness for

our sin. It is important to forgive others. Jesus virtually gave us a blank checkbook on anything we wanted in God. Mark 11:23 - 25 says, "Truly I tell you, if you say to this mountain, 'Be taken up and thrown into the sea' and if you do not doubt in your heart, but believe that what you say will come to pass, it will be done for you. So I tell you whatever you ask for in prayer, believe that you have received it, and it will be yours. WHENEVER YOU STAND PRAYING, FORGIVE, if you have anything against anyone; SO THAT YOUR FATHER IN HEAVEN MAY ALSO FORGIVE YOU your trespasses." (NRSV) This blank check is good, but, it is contingent on forgiving others. It is also important to forgive yourself. If you have given your sins to God, let the forgiveness you have received by faith, fill your being with the freedom and joy of being forgiven. Don't beat up on yourself anymore. In Corinthians 5:17 we see, "So if anyone is in Christ, there is a new creation: everything old has passed away; see, everything has become new!" (NRSV) (Used by permission)

(Dr. Abshier is a well known physician in Portland, Oregon.)

Sin is sand in the wheels of life. There can be no lasting peace nor deep felt joy within where sin is allowed to remain. Jesus came, died and was resurrected so that we could be saved from sin and placed into a loving relationship with God. If we try to hide our sins we cannot prosper, the scripture tells us.

But if we confess our sins God is faithful to forgive us our sins and cleans us from all unrighteousness. (IJohn 1:9) He will take away our "un-rightness" and establish us in a right relationship with God and with our fellow man. And also with ourselves!

The Psalmist said, "Search me, O God, and know my heart: try me, and know my thoughts: And see if there be any wicked way in me, and lead me in the way everlasting." (Ps. 139:23-24)

And again in Psalms 101:1 & 2 he says, "I will sing about your loving kindness and your justice, Lord. I will sing your praises! ...I will try to walk a blameless path, but how I need your help, especially in my own home, where I long to act as I should." Living Bible

This is right where we live! Our own home is our best testing ground. We need God's help, especially there!

The book of Psalms is rich with human experience and it speaks to us all. It is a very good prayer book to use in your quiet time. Ask the Holy Spirit to minister to your soul as you read it. He will nurture you like a loving, tender parent. He is rich in love and compassion. He is the Love of God reaching down to God's children. Learn to lean on him for healing of wounds, for strength in weakness, and for wisdom during confusing times.

Oh how precious is the Holy Spirit!! Feel his warm-hearted love. He will bring peace, joy, wisdom and honor to your life. His blessings will make you rich with a wealth this world knows nothing of. He will make your heart sing praises to the Father, to the son and to the Holy Spirit.

Amen and amen. It is so!

CHAPTER 12
PRAYER FORMULA

Here is a brief formula for prayer. You may use it to start your own spirit flowing.

1. PRAISE: Psalms 92:1-5. Living Bible

It is good to say, "Thank you" to the Lord, to sing praises to the God who is above all gods. Every morning tell him, "Thank you for your kindness," and every evening rejoice in all his faithfulness. Sing his praises, accompanied by music... You have done so much for me, O Lord. No wonder I am glad! I sing for joy. O Lord, what miracles you do! And how deep are your thoughts!

2. THANKSGIVING: Psalms 136:1-9 and 138:1-3. LB

O Give thanks to the Lord for he is good: his loving kindness continues forever.

Lord, with all my heart I thank you. I will sing your praises before the armies of angels in heaven. I face your Temple as I worship, giving thanks to you for all your loving kindness, for your promises are backed by all the honor of your name. When I pray, you answer me, and encourage me by giving me the strength I need.

3. CONFESSION. Psalms 51:1-3 and 10-12

O Loving and kind God, have mercy. Have pity upon me and take away the awful stain of my transgressions. Oh, wash me, cleanse me from this guilt. Let me be pure again. For I admit my shameful deed--it haunts me day and night. ...(6) You deserve honesty from the heart; yes, utter sincerity and truthfulness. Oh give me this wisdom...(10) Create in me a new, clean heart, O God, filled with clean thoughts and right desires...(12) Restore to me again the joy of your salvation, and make me willing to obey you.

4. MEDITATION: Psalms 42:1&2a Ps. 46:10 KJV
Ps. 37:4 & 5 LB

As the deer pants for water, so I long for you O God. I thirst for God, the living God.

Be still and know that I am God: ...I will be exalted in all the earth.

Be delighted with the Lord. Then he will give you all your heart's desires. Commit everything you do to the Lord. Trust him to help you do it and he will.

5. SUPPLICATION AND INTERCESSION: (Prayer for yourself and for others) Psalms 31:1-3, 21&22, 24.

Lord, I trust in you alone. Don't let my enemies defeat me. Rescue me because you are the God who always does what is right. Answer quickly when I cry to you; bend low and hear my whispered plea. Be for me a great Rock of safety from my foes. Yes you are my Rock and my fortress; honor your name by leading me out of this peril.... Into your hands I commit my spirit.

Blessed is the Lord, for he has shown me that his never-failing love protects me like the walls of a fort! I spoke too hastily when I said, "The Lord has deserted me," for you listened to my plea and answered me...

So cheer up! Take courage if you are depending on the Lord.

As you read these Bible verses, you will be led to other scriptures which will enrich your soul. Give God the time he needs to teach and nurture you. Admit to Jesus that you are a babe of his spirit. Let him nurture you as you would care for a baby of your earth-body.

He is more loving, more caring, more wise and more compassionate than any earthly mother could ever be.

CHAPTER 13
YOUR GREATEST FRIEND

Feel free to talk to Jesus about whatever is on your mind. Allow him to be your best friend and trust him. He will not condemn you when you open your heart to him. Listen for the still, small voice within you. If it is good and wise, that's Jesus talking to you. Always remember that Jesus wants to have an intimate relationship with you.

He wants to be your dear friend. We develop friendships with people by spending time with them and talking with them. Do your part to build a friendship with Jesus and you can be sure Jesus will do his part. Each day take time to meet him. No friendship can grow without time and attention. The more you're with someone you like the stronger your friendship becomes.

When I fell in love with my husband, I couldn't quit talking about him. I couldn't quit thinking about him. When you fall in love with Jesus the same will happen to you. Ask him to help you to love him dearly.

Think about the goodness, the gentleness of Jesus. Think of all the love he came to give and what he sacrificed to do it. Think of the fact that he loves you, personally. Sense him sitting or walking beside you. Feel his love and say to him, "Jesus, I'm so glad you love me. I love you, too." And reflect his love to others. Smile at them and mentally say, "Jesus loves you and me." "I'm so glad Jesus loves you and me." If you do this consistently you will surely fall in love with Jesus.

My daughter, Marydith, had some insurmountable problems. She talked to Jesus about them and Jesus said, "Praise me. Keep praising me. Keep thanking me." The thought was to say "Thank you Jesus. Thank you Jesus. Thank you Jesus."

Marydith felt uncomfortable saying it again and again. The still, small voice said to her mind, "Say it anyway." She did. She said it over and over again. Soon a peace came to her which parted the dark clouds above. This great peace lingered in her mind and heart. In time God guided her to a desirable solution to her problems.

The Bible says, "It is a good thing to give thanks unto the Lord." Ps. 92:1

I have found that thankfulness is very good medicine, especially for depression. It brings a "merry heart." And "A merry heart doeth good like a medicine," The Bible says. (Ps. 17:22)

Here is a potent affirmation. Repeat it over and over again until it becomes a part of your thinking. You'll find it uplifting and that it releases stress.

All glory and honor, wisdom and power are in you, oh God. You are in Christ. I live in Christ and Christ lives in me.
    Thank You Jesus!
    Thank you Jesus!
    Thank you Jesus!

As you continue to affirm this it will take its place in your conscious mind and, in time, it will sink into your subconscious.

It will then flow out from you. The circulation of Christ-life will flow to enrich you and your surroundings. In this way your spirit will bear its fruit. This is dwelling in Christ and letting him dwell in you.

He says if we do so, we will bear much fruit and our joy will be full. Wisdom, love and power flow from the Father God through Jesus to you, but you must be open to receive it.

When you allow Christ to dwell within, you will have power for everything that is good, noble, and true. As the fifteenth chapter of John tells us, this power continues to flow through us when we stay attached to the vine, Christ Jesus. But we, the branches, must be surrendered to the vine. If a branch wills to bend or twist or break, the flow of Christ's spirit will be hindered or cut off.

The choice is ours, mine and yours.

If you want to find God in everyday living, then every day you must be open to the flow of his Spirit.

CHAPTER 14
LOVE OF YOUR GOD WITHIN

In Phillipians the Apostle Paul says, "That I might know him..." This was my cry, "Lord Jesus, that I might know you; that I might be made right in you, sense your Presence, believe you truly are with me and in me. With my whole heart I desire a sweet, day to day friendship with you."

I was hungry to read books by people who knew God. B. A. Tozer's book, *The Pursuit Of God*, was one of them. On page 12 he describes the kind of religion I first had. He says, "The whole transaction of religious conversion has been made mechanical and spiritless..... Christ may be 'received' without creating any special love for him in the soul of the receiver." (That was me.)

My conversion consisted of being good in outward actions. I managed not to curse, smoke, drink, dance or have pre- or extra- marital sex. I didn't even allow myself to think dirty thoughts or to lust. I didn't go to movies because my church was against it. But I did not have joy in my religion. I certainly didn't have a friendship with Jesus. I did not know him in an intimate, personal way. Nor did I have the love of God within me.

I understood that God's love was great and wide and deep

and strong. But the knowledge was in my head. That love was outside of me, and it was beyond me. Love my enemies? No, not me. (Really, I tried. I wanted to, but I just couldn't do it.)

The following spurred me on.

Tozer writes, "Religion, so far as it is genuine, is in essence the response of created personalities (that's us) to the Creating Personality, God. 'This is life eternal, that they might know thee the only true God, and Jesus Christ, whom thou hast sent.'

"God is a Person, and in the deep of His High Mighty Nature He thinks, wills, enjoys, feels, loves, desires and suffers as any other person may. In making himself known to us He stays by the familiar pattern of personality. He communicates with us through the avenues of our minds, our wills and our emotions. The continuous and unembarrassed interchange of love and thought between God and the soul of the redeemed man is the throbbing heart of New Testament religion."

What a statement! What a God Tozer knows! That's the kind of God I wanted to know, one with a personality who feels and hurts, too; one who communicates with me through my mind, my will and my emotions in an interchange of love; a God who is alive in all the ways I am alive!

I will seek him! I thought. *I will pray for a heart-hunger for him! I will ask Jesus to guide me to him.*

Then I found this scripture, "Thou shalt seek me and find me when thou shalt search for me with all thine heart." It said to me, "Adele, you can find God. So begin your whole-hearted search!"

I prayed, "God, help me to search for you with all my heart. I want to know you, Lord Jesus, in your personality, in your communication, in your 'interchange of love' and 'thought with my soul!'"

When I sought God with my whole heart, he did a most

beautiful thing for me. It was beyond my imaginings. Never had I experienced anything like it in my whole life. As I knelt in prayer, he sent his Spirit, who breathed into me as a fragrant, gentle breeze and blew all the bitterness out of my heart. It was beyond comprehension, description or expression.

From that moment on, God was my deepest heart's desire.

CHAPTER 15
FOR THE JOY OF LIVING

You will find it is imperative to seek God as a friend in order to find him for the joy of your everyday living, for answers to your needs and help with your problems.

He hears when we ask for things. Many times he will grant them as a father does for a son. But our hearts will never know the great peace and joy in living until we want Jesus for himself alone - until we want a love relationship with the Lover of our souls.

How can we have a warm friendship with someone whom we neglect? Jesus cannot feel welcome in a heart that neglects him. And surely not in one that is full of bitterness and anger.

This truth was demonstrated strongly in the lives of my husband's grandparents. Once they were Christians but now they were mean, angry people who were, according to Sam, "at each other all the time."

None of the family seems to know just what it was in their lives that caused the bitterness and anger to grow. But they became caustically angry and bitter toward each other.

One time Grandma made a delicious fried chicken dinner. She set the table for herself and Sam's Aunt Lillian, who was living with them. The two sat down and filled their plates with mashed potatoes, fried chicken, gravy, and greens. In Grandpa's plate Grandma put a cob of dry corn she brought up from the barn. It was the same corn they fed to the hogs. He treated her in kind.

Another day, Grandpa came home from picking a bucket full of wild blackberries. Planning to can them, he went down to the fruit cellar to get jars. There he discovered Grandma had filled all the jars with her home-grown cabbage for sauerkraut.

Without regard for Grandma and her much work, Grandpa opened the jars, pulled out the kraut and dumped it into a bucket. Grandma came down and caught him. They argued bitterly. In hot anger, Grandma grabbed Grandpa's big, shaggy beard and gave it a hard yank. That infuriated, Grandpa, and with his hand on a kraut jar, he hit Grandma over the head.

Enraged, Grandma stomped up the stone steps of the fruit cellar, down the dirt path and into the white, frame farm house. She hurriedly packed a bag, clutched it in her angry fist and walked down the long lane, never to return.

Years later, Sam was at the farm, sitting with Grandpa on a wooden bench outside the screened-in back porch.

With deep reflection in Grandpa's voice he said, "Sammy, it was the saddest day of my life when I saw Grandma walking down that lane. I'd rather have seen her go by in a hearse. I know she could be a mean old lady, but she had her good points, too. And I loved her."

"Grandpa!" Sam said, startled by this confession, "Why didn't you run after her and tell her you were sorry?"

"Ohhh noooo," drawled Grandpa, "I could never do that."

What was this anger and meanness that provoked two people who loved each other to be so hateful?

Jesus told us. It is a root of bitterness grown to possess the soul. The power of Satan had taken over their lives. As we have seen, the Scripture tells us "Satan is like a roaring lion going about the earth seeking whom he may devour." He devoured Grandma and Grandpa.

In Grandpa's older years he asked Sam's mother and father to live with him and take care of the farm. After moving in, they noticed Grandpa's anger was so intense he was taking it out on the livestock. He beat the cows unmercifully with a club when they swished their tails on him while he milked. Any farmer knows it's natural for cows to swipe flies off themselves with their tails.

Once Grandpa was so mad at a horse he hit her in the head and blinded one of her eyes. Angry at another horse, he grabbed its head in his arms and almost bit its ear off. Finally Grandpa was forbidden to be near the livestock.

Toward the end of his life Sam's mother was caring for Grandpa. She knew he was very ill and close to death. He had been in bed for several days, too sick to get up. Now he wanted to go outdoors.

Mother said, "No, Pa. You're too sick to do that. You need to stay in bed and take care of yourself."

With his usual anger Grandpa yelled, "You're just trying to make a prisoner out of me. I'm not that sick!"

"You're mistaken, Pa," Mother said. "You're sicker than you think."

Grandpa got up anyway. He was putting on his trousers. With one foot in his trouser leg he let out a heinous cry, "Aw! I guess I am mistaken. I guess I've been mistaken in a lot of things!" And he slumped to the floor and died.

The hold Satan had on Grandpa convinced me early in my adult life that I did not want to live out my years in anger. I would do whatever was needed to find release from my anger.

I don't know what problems you're wrestling with. But if

you are not enjoying Abundant Life, Satan is working to keep you from it. Jesus will help you identify your problems and help you solve them. Ask him. Listen to him. Obey him. That's the formula for success.

Jesus promised to give "Joy Unspeakable."

The Psalmist David said, "Search me oh God and know my heart; test me and know my thoughts. See if there be any wicked way in me, and lead me in the way everlasting." (Ps. 139:23 & 24)

Often we don't know what it is in our subconscious mind that is rankling our spirits. Sometimes we've lived with a certain tendency so long it feels natural, like it's a part of us. If you are hurting because of something someone has done to you or said about you it's important that you take that very thing to God in prayer. Tell God about it and ask him what you should do to clear the matter up. Don't let things fester within you. The Bible speaks of a root of bitterness. Don't let that root grow into a tree like Grandpa did. It possessed his whole life. And why let anything siphon off your joy of living?

If you have something against another person be willing to ask the person about it. Maybe no harm was intended. But if there was, be willing to forgive them. The Holy Spirit who is in you will guide you. Listen for his guidance and don't be afraid to act on it. He will go before you and prepare the way for you.

Pray the prayer which King David did. Ask God to search your innermost being. Be honest with God. If he brings something to your attention, Please, Please don't cover it up. It will only fester and grow. Ask Jesus to help you face it. Ask him to guide you in addressing it. Be courageous. Fight the good fight of faith.

Be careful not to seek revenge. Be willing to take blame. This is the humble path that leads to the high road. Believe me when I say Jesus will honor your honesty and humility. He surely, surely will!

Keep praying, "Create in me a clean heart Oh God and renew a right spirit within me." You will be abundantly blessed. This is a promise, I say it again, You will be abundantly blessed with the joy of living!

CHAPTER 16
SWEET PEACE THROUGH FORGIVENESS

As noted earlier, Sam's grandma was as mean as his grandpa.

When Sam and his siblings were young she would come to their house to help mend clothes. If one of the children didn't do exactly as she thought they should, she would beat them unmercifully. They were all afraid of her.

I've never understood why Sam's mother allowed it. She probably knew, if she crossed Grandma, that would be the end of their relationship.

Grandma was mean, stubborn, and rebellious against God and the church. Sam's parents continued to look after her needs and loved her. Often they invited her to go to church with them. But to no avail. Regardless of the love of God and the goodness Sam's parents showed, Grandma remained stubbornly resisting.

After Sam and I graduated from Pacific Bible College (now Warner Pacific College) we went back to Sam's hometown, Carthage, Missouri. There the pastor of Sam's boyhood church asked him to conduct a two-week revival meeting.

In the evenings when Sam preached I felt bad that his grandmother was not at church to hear him. I felt she would feel so proud of him.

One time I suggested we invite Grandma and Aunt Lillian

to go to church with us. Sam said, "They won't go. Mom and Dad have invited them and offered to drive them to church. The family has invited them to church so many times, they don't even like to be asked any more."

But this particular day I insisted. To my surprise Grandma said she'd go.

"She just says that to get rid of us," Sam told me. "You'll see. When we get there she'll tell us she changed her mind or she isn't feeling well. She's done it so many times that it's a pattern."

When we walked up the three wooden steps of the small, white, wooden frame house, there to Sam's surprise, was Grandma, hair slicked back into a bun, dressed in a flowered, pink, cotton dress and pleasantly ready to go to church.

In church she sat beside me on a pew near the front. Sam had Grandma's full attention while he preached. At the end of his sermon he invited people to come kneel at the altar who wanted to give their hearts to the Lord Jesus.

"I would love to pray with you," Sam said warmly to the congregation.

I noticed Grandma was trembling and clutching the back of the pew in front of us. "Grandma," I whispered, "if you'd like to go to the altar, I'll go with you."

"I would like to," were her simple words.

I was surprised to hear them come out of her mouth as calmly and deliberately as any thing I'd ever heard her say. We walked down the aisle together and knelt at the wooden altar where Sam, as a ten-year-old, gave his heart to the Lord.

Sam came and knelt on the other side of Grandma. They had a brief conversation and Sam led Grandma in a repentant prayer. Tears streamed down her face as she accepted Jesus and his forgiveness.

The next evening she was very willing to come to church with us. After singing some congregational hymns, the pastor invited testimonies from the congregation. Grandma was the first to stand. In a more kindly voice than Sam or I had ever heard, Grandma said, "Last night I gave my heart to the Lord. I went home and slept like a baby. That's the first good night's sleep I've had in thirty years. I'm so glad my grandson, Sammy, came back to preach for us."

Grandma was a new person. She wrote a letter to each of Sam's sisters whom she had beaten so cruelly and asked them to forgive her. She told them she gave her heart to the Lord and she wanted to make things right with them and with God.

Jesus said, "I have overcome the world." When it seems the world's condition is hopeless and Satan is rampant, there is a power available to the humble, yielded heart. It is God's power of forgiveness, love and new-life.

Again, if you have a problem which you haven't been able to solve, and if you want to have the peace, joy and guidance to live an abundant life, you will find God and his power to release you and fulfill your life when you seek him with your whole heart.

We know Grandma's enjoying the place Jesus went to prepare for us. We wish we could be sure of the same for Grandpa.

CHAPTER 17
HIDDEN SINS/DEEP CLEANSING

Sometimes we surrender a part of our lives to Jesus and don't even know there are "hidden sins" in our heart which Jesus wants us to recognize and surrender.

Just such a thing happened to me one day. After many years of enjoying an intimate friendship with Jesus, I hit a plateau in my relationship with him. Life had become humdrum. The freshness was gone. I no longer felt the excitement and joy of living.

When I became aware of it I remembered, "The way up in the Kingdom of God is down - down on your knees in humility." Down on my knees I went, back to seeking the Lord with my whole heart. My "repentant prayer" position was one of "knees and nose to the floor." There I humbly prayed, "Jesus, please restore to me the joy of my salvation and the sweetness of my friendship with you."

Then I heard that still, small voice say, "Repent."

"Repent?" I wondered, "Repent of what? Have I sinned?" I couldn't recall a rebellious act or word for which I should feel guilty.

"Repent," came the quiet command again.

"All right, Lord Jesus, I will repent. I will repent of anything you bring to my mind whether I remember committing it or not. If I haven't done it, I will pray a repentant prayer for the one who has. I will be a worker with you to redeem another by urgent, intercessory prayer."

In sincere prayer I asked for forgiveness for every sin that came to my mind. I prayed for the prostitute as though I had been one, for the murderer as though I had committed the murder, for the thief as though I had been a robber. In deep repentance I prayed.

Then strangely, I heard these words, "Repent of your wit."

"My wit?!" I said in shock.

"Repent of my wit? My humor? Surely humor isn't sinful. Isn't humor the oil on the wheels of life? Could it be sinful, Lord?" I asked.

I waited for an answer.

"Repent of your wit." Again it came.

It was not a strong, judgmental voice. It was the calm, gentle voice I had come to recognize as my Loving Lord. But why would he tell me to repent of something I felt was one of my best qualities? My friends would often laugh when I didn't even think of being funny.

I knew I was mischievous. But I never tried to hurt people with my humor, or so I assumed.

"Repent of your wit," remained in my mind.

"All right, Lord. I don't understand it at all, but if you ask me to repent of my wit, I don't have to understand. I only have to obey. I will humbly repent of my wit."

"Lord Jesus," I said, "forgive me for my humor."

"Cast it on the cross."

What was I hearing? It was the same, steady, calm voice speaking.

Now I was shocked!

"Cast my humor, my wit, my fun-loving nature on the cross? But Lord, that's my best quality."

"Cast it on the cross," came the calm message again.

I writhed in confusion and in pain. Was Jesus asking me to crucify my personality? Humor is one thing I love. It seemed he was asking me to destroy my personality.

The more I thought about it the more I agonized. It was like killing one of my beloved pets or even my own dear child! I thought I couldn't do it. But I had already learned the lesson of absolute surrender. And so, like Abraham took Isaac to the mountain I fortified myself to take this little child of my person to it's death.

"Help me! Oh Lord Jesus, help me!" I cried. "I will die for you, if you ask me to. But oh, you must help me!"

With that I reached my hand into my heart and (in imagery of mind) I tore this little fun loving person out of my being and thrust her. Like a living doll I thrust her on the cross. Quickly I grabbed a spike and drove it through her breast, nailing her there lest she fly right back to me.

Then I wept my heart out at the loss of this, my beloved little one.

I wept and wept as I grieved, "My little Adele is gone, dead, crucified." With my knees and my nose on the gold-colored carpet in our living room, I wept in utter grief and sorrow.

"I did it for you, Lord Jesus. But only you know why I was asked to do it," I prayed when I could compose myself.

"Look up, Child," came the tender voice.

I lifted my wet face off the damp carpet and with spiritual eyes looked at the cross. There hung the doll I loved so much. It was "me;" round, happy face with big blue eyes.

But something was happening to it.

The soft, round cheeks began to sag. Then the skin drooped

and sagged in deep folds.

Now the flesh sloughed off.

I watched with amazement as I noticed this sweet, happy face was only a facade! Underneath it was a grotesque figure. And the ugly, cruel face of a demon snarled at me.

I recognized it. I recognized it as the spirit in which I could put someone down when I thought he or she needed it.

Now I was speechless.

When I recovered, I said, "But Lord, I thought I was doing you service. Some people need to be put in their places, don't they?"

"Child," Jesus said, "that is the work of the Holy Spirit. It is never a duty assigned to my children. Your assignment is always to speak in love and truth, with compassion."

"I see, Lord, I see. Cleanse me and help me to remember."

Now I do remember. And smartingly well! The incident so shocked, jarred and pained me that I cannot forget it. I pray God help me to forever remember my place and the place of gentle, godly humor in my relationships.

"Love never puts people down." Jesus told me, "Love never cuts or crushes. It always lifts and blesses with tenderness, lightness and joy."

"I thank you. I praise you," my spirit shouted. "Lord Jesus, how long suffering and kind you have been with me. You didn't show me my wrong when I was young and tender. You waited until my soul was tougher and could handle it. How I praise you!!

"And Jesus, I do not want ever to house one of Satan's henchmen. No, not one! Show me my heart so I can repent. Cleanse me from every unrighteous way."

"The sacrifice acceptable to God is a broken spirit; a broken and contrite heart, Oh God, wilt thou not despise." (Ps. 51:17)

The Bible says God loves a broken heart. He will heal it to be a cheerful heart. If you want God's joy in your everyday living you must seek him in the deep recesses of your soul. He wants to live there to replace every unlovely thing. He wills to fill you with pure love, joy and peace.

How refreshing I found a deep cleansing to be!

CHAPTER 18
WORKING WITH GOD

"Happy are those who put their trust in God," the Bible tells us. (Ps. 40:4)

Recently I was talking with a young man who has long been a close friend of our grandsons, Brett and Joshua. Because he did not relate well to his own family, he latched onto ours. Johnny is a fine young man and we enjoy having him around.

His car clunked out and he was going to buy a truck to use for work. He told me he had two trucks in mind and that he was going to look at them again the next day.

Since I was going to help him financially I said, "Honey, promise me one thing; you will not buy a vehicle until you feel here in your heart that it is the one God has for you." With that I tapped Johnny's chest over his heart. "I'm going to pray with you now and ask God to direct you to the very truck that is right for you."

Standing in the driveway alongside our house, we bowed our heads together. I said a prayer asking God to guide Johnny to the truck that would serve him well in his work and give him pleasure. That was what Johnny wanted. He agreed he would listen carefully for God's guidance.

On his noon hour the next day Johnny went to the car lot to

look at the two trucks. One was already purchased and gone. He walked over to the other. The salesman extolled the virtues of the truck as they stood outside on that warm, cloudless, spring day. But suddenly, out of a clear sky, it rained down on Johnny's head.

Johnny later told me, "I wondered then if that was God saying something to me. But all this was kinda new to me so I kept on looking at the truck. Pretty soon it began to hail. Then hail peppered down on me real hard. I figured someone was talking to me, and I said to the salesman, 'I don't think I'd better take this truck.'

"'Wait! Stay here,' the salesman urged, 'I'm going in to see the boss. I think I can get you a better deal.'

"Immediately the hale peppered down harder.

"The salesman came out saying, 'I'm going to knock $500 off the price.'

"At that very moment," Johnny said, "I slipped on a small piece of hail and fell to the ground. That was unusual for me. You know how quick I am on my feet.

"Oh oh, I thought, Someone's telling me not to buy this truck. I'd better get out of here before I get struck by lightning. And I left the salesman standing with his mouth open.

"I went home after work, and called a man about a Toyota truck I saw advertised in the newspaper. As soon as I heard the man's voice, a good feeling came over me. When we took the truck for a test drive, I mentioned hearing a slight rattle.

"'Let's go to the garage and have a mechanic look at it.' the man said without hesitation.

"When we got there, the mechanic pulled up the hood, stuck his head in and came out saying, 'It's just a slightly loose timing chain. I tightened it.'

"The sound was gone. I liked the little truck. I felt real good to be driving it. And I bought it for the exact amount I had planned on paying for a truck."

Johnny continued, "I like the looks of the dark blue-metallic body so I'll enjoy washing it, too. And the best thing of all, I know it's the one God wanted me to buy."

The story of Johnny's new truck illustrates the lesson I had learned from Dr. E. Stanley Jones. "Listen, learn, obey."

Again, these are the three main steps in establishing a fulfilling relationship with Jesus. Here I had the joy of passing these steps on to Johnny, one of God's younger children. I do think a relationship with Jesus is the most fun in all the world! And if you practice trusting God in the constant you will find him more easily in the crises.

CHAPTER 19
DON'T WORRY? REALLY, NOW!

Listen. Learn. Obey.

How simple it sounds. But it isn't that simple to understand these three essentials and to live by them day by day. I was willing to do all three and I wanted to learn them well. Over and over again I practiced this, that E. Stanley Jones told me to do. I listened in the silence of my soul to hear the voice of God. And I tried to learn as I stove to obey the Lord.

Father Fenelon, for centuries the Spiritual teacher of many noted Christians, says, "This voice is not a stranger there. God is in our souls as our souls are in our bodies."

I tried to form a habit of pausing to ask Jesus what he wanted me to do and to learn from each difficult situation that I faced. I asked him to guide me and to help me obey his directions.

Then, as I was reading in Phillipians chapter four, verse six, a new command hit me. Although I had read it many times before I just glazed over it. Now I had to look at it. St. Paul, the great Biblical writer, told me not to worry about anything.

"That's a biggy!" I said to the Apostle, "Whoever has accomplished that?!"

My accusative resistance didn't change the Scripture any. So I said, "All right. I'll practice."

I began by checking my fretfulness. When I worried I confessed it as sin and I told God about my problem. I envisioned myself putting my concern into God's big outstretched hands. Whenever my thoughts went to the problem, again I submitted it to God. Over and over again I practiced letting go of my worrying. Too, I listened intently to hear that still, small voice within telling me what to do. I did my best to act on the message given and then to let the matter rest.

Very recently I was tested and shown my poor progress.

A big upset happened in some very important plans I had made. In my ignorance of the details I made a hasty decision. It was a mistake. I thought I was doing the right thing. But I wasn't. And my plans were aborted. I was so very disappointed that I grieved over it.

Now I know you, my reader, are curious to know what those big plans were. I hesitate to confess this, but I will.

As a novice in the publishing world, I misunderstood the price a publisher gave me to publish our last book. He was a Christian and I took the first price he said as a final word. Then when we had agreed for his company to print the book the new and final price he quoted was a fourth higher. I thought it unfair and spoke to him about it, suggesting as a Christian I felt he should keep his word. Of course, he didn't appreciate that. (Small wonder.) He said he first quoted an approximate price and then suggested I find a publisher that was closer to home. (His company is in St. Louis, Missouri.) When I went back over our correspondences I found he was right. The price he quoted was approximate. I was wrong. And since I had told others of the "good deal" we were getting, I was embarrassed and humiliated to have to tell them differently.

I tried to mend the brokenness, but the other party would not agree.

I was greatly disappointed, even to the emotional state of grief, depression and physical pain. Not only was my ego decidedly bruised but my plans were aborted. I had to start all over again to find a publisher and work out a plan with him. This ate up the time we had left and would keep us from having the books by our State Camp Meeting time.

Of course, one of the first things I did was pray. "Oh God, help me to correct this broken situation." I made several calls of apology with polite pleading but nothing changed the man's mind.

I grieved the more.

Finally, When I looked into the mirror and saw my sad countenance my reflection looked back at me and said, "You don't have to be sad. Confess your fault to the Lord and let him heal you and the situation, too."

"Lord," I said, "please heal this situation. I know you can give me another chance. You can even make it better than the first. You can take my foolishness and cause it to do me good. You can bring beauty out of ashes."

I felt God say, "I will bless you. I will bring good out of brokenness. Trust me."

So I surrendered to whatever God would do with it, "Lord I put all things into your hands. I trust you to bless this project and even make it bring glory to your name. Amen"

With that surrender and statement of trust, peace came.

And to my surprise, a bigger blessing came with God's dealings of the situation than I could ever have imagined.

My nephew has a printing company and together we produced a beautiful book and got it out in the nick of time for Camp Meeting. Through this plan God reached into my family and touched lives with love, joy and a witness of Himself. These lives would not have been encountered in this way without my big "boo boo." And the whole project became fun, especially with the warm, friendship times I had with my nephew and his family.

I've told others, "God will get right down in your worst grungies with you and make a beautiful clay pot out of your mud." He did just that for me! And with gusto!

(Praise you Jesus!)

I am still learning, both how to behave better and how to get out of an emotional funk more quickly.

By the way, I did write a letter of apology to the first publisher and sent him a two pound box of See's Chocolates. He called to tell me I was forgiven and thanked me for the candy, but said I hadn't needed to send it. Well, I felt better for doing so.

CHAPTER 20
GOD'S GOT RAINBOWS

One of the greatest concerns of Sam's and my life was a health problem Sam had. It plagued him for years and caused us great anxiety. We went to many doctors and to several noted clinics. None could diagnose his case.

His symptoms? For one, he had headaches that incapacitated him. One day he was out visiting the sick. When he got back into the car he noticed he could not feel the steering wheel in his hands. He hit his face. No feeling there. I'd better go home, he thought. But now let's see, how do I get home?

He couldn't remember the way.

I'll go ask at that service station.

He drove across the highway to the service station but couldn't speak coherently. How he got home he couldn't remember.

That evening Wednesday prayer meeting was at the church. He was leading it when, again, he got dizzy, his head ached furiously and his speech was incoherent. Awkwardly he explained to the people that he was sick and asked me to take over.

When I got home I asked him what was the matter. He said, "Don't ask me anything. My head aches so bad I can't think.

You can talk to me but please don't ask me a question."

Whether Sam's symptoms were the result of his head being crushed under the wheels of a car when he was a youngster or some other condition we never did find out.

When he was miserable we were all miserable.

Some time after that, Sam and I were coming home from Clarksburg, California where we visited our son, Grant, and his family. Sam was driving. He was in a heavy, depressed mood. He wasn't talking or interacting with me. Almost zombie like he drove the car. I was lying down in the back seat thinking, worrying and praying.

I said, "Oh God help us. You know how unhappy we are."

In my inner self I heard the words, "Look up child. I have given you rainbows."

With that I rose up in the back seat and looked out the windshield. In the distance, across the sky, from the earth on the right of the highway to the earth on the left, there arched the biggest, brightest triple rainbow. Three rainbows! One bright, wonderfully beautiful bow right on top of the other! Biggest I'd ever seen before and never have I seen one like it since. Each arch was distinct in every color as though the artist was standing right there with his big brush swishing it across the sky in band after band of exciting hue.

I gasped! "Oh God, if you really have that beauty for my life I will trust and be content."

From then on I watched and waited for my rainbows. They didn't come. Then I wavered and I quavered as I waited longer and longer. Rainbows did not come. They did not come. And they did not come. For years no rainbows came. My faith was not steady. I doubted, Did God really talk to me or was it all my own wishful thinking?

Often I asked, "God, didn't you say you would give me

rainbows?"

Then one day, after many years of pain, toil, heartache, worry and fretting, God started to brush my skies with rainbows. He put so much color in my sky I could hardly believe it. The church gifted us with travels to the Holy Lands, mission fields, Europe and elsewhere overseas. They caringly looked after our retirement. God blessed us both with health. He gave me the home I desired and finances to share. And one day, one unusual day---

Sam's sister called us from New Smyrna Beach, Florida and said to Sam, "Would you like a Cadillac?"

Sam said, "Would I like a Cadillac?!!"

"If you'll come and get mine, you can have it. I can't drive it and I don't need the money so I don't want to sell it."

Sam's sister, Roberta, whom we call Bertie, is legally blind and, of course, cannot drive a car. Her husband died shortly after they bought this new Cadillac. It had eight thousand miles on it.

"Now it's filling up my garage," Bertie said, "and I'd like to use the space."

When Sam and I got off the plane, there was Bertie and Sam's brother, Bob, to whom she had already given money to buy a BMW. Bertie dangled the gold keys in front of Sam's face and said, "Here Honey, yours with love. Take and enjoy."

That was a thrill. But it was not the biggest band of color in my rainbow. The biggest and brightest was that God blessed Sam and me both with health. At seventy nine (me) and eighty-one (Sam) at the time of this writing, neither of us are on prescription medication. We walk a mile and a half each morning (usually) at Clackamas Town Center Mall, take care of our house and yard and enjoy each other's friendship more than anything in the world other than our love relationship with

Jesus.

Another wonderful rainbow is that God turned events so miraculously that our wonderful grandson, Nick, and his darling wife, Nicola, were able to buy the house directly behind ours. Our yards meet at a gated fence. Sam made a lovely, flower strewn garden path from our back door to theirs. They are sheer joy; warm, loving and caring. We have great fun together. What a brilliant rainbow God gave me!!

And the very fact that Jesus loves us and we love him a whole big bunch puts a bright rainbow in my sky every day!

One day I was praying in my quiet time and Jesus said to me, "Did I give you rainbows?"

"Oh yes! yes! yes!yes!yes!" I shouted in the quiet of my mind and heart. "Yes oh yes, God, you did! You surely did give me rainbows! Oh I praise you! Yes God, You Gave Me Rainbows!"

Do you want rainbows? God is no respecter of persons. Seek him with an honest, sincere heart - your whole heart. Endure the hardships he allows and learn from them.

Trust him.

He's got lotsa rainbows!!!

An after thought: Just this past Christmas our son, Randy, bought his wife, Jenni, a BMW and she gave me her Mercedes. Here we are, two "poor preachers"(Just an expression. We're not poor!) driving a couple prestigious cars. Now that's funny!! Who says God doesn't have a sense of humor - and lotsa rainbows?!

CHAPTER 21
PRAY WITHOUT CEASING?

The Apostle Paul instructs us to "Pray without ceasing."
Early on that was a scripture I couldn't understand.

How could one do that? I questioned. Can I stay on my knees all day? Do I have to keep my mind unengaged in my daily chores so that I can think of saying prayers to God all day? Maybe unceasing prayer is only for monks or preachers whose job it is.

Then through the years I developed an awareness of Jesus being with me at all times. Every beautiful thing I see, hear, or think provokes me to say, "Thank you, Jesus."

I've come to realize in my inner being, the truth of the scripture which says, "Every good and perfect gift comes from the father of lights in whom is no variableness neither shadow of turning." And so everything, but everything, good reminds me of Jesus! When he's there, as he always is, it's natural for me to thank him as I would out of habit thank anyone else who did me a favor. Now I realize, that, too, is praying.

When I see, hear, or think of a hurtful thing, it is just as natural for me to say, "God help!" or "God bless!" A siren rarely sounds within my hearing but what I send a prayer, "Be with that person, Lord Jesus. May they feel your Presence near them."

Or maybe I'll ask that the person's angel will be close by to guide and direct all who are involved. In my mind's eye I see the attendants as angels of the Lord in mercy ministering to the patient. Sometimes I ask that the doctor who will tend the patient be guided by Jesus' Spirit, that the surgeon's hands be guided by God. That's praying - without ceasing.

Just as it takes years for a concert pianist to roll his fingers across the keys without thought of the notes, so a constant practice of prayer makes a heart-felt flight of thought toward heaven natural.

So, to pray without ceasing is natural for me now. I could not cease to pray. The very thought of it shivers me. Oh how poverty stricken I would be if I could not pray always!

My deep heart's desire is that there may be a sacramental quality to my every day living. By that I mean, as the apostle Paul says, "In him we live and move and have our being." I want to sacrifice my life to Jesus to live through me. Could there possibly be a better choice for one's life, for one's relationships, for one's activities? I think not.

Then what do we have to do?

We must be honest, honest with ourselves and with God.

This Christ who is truth, love, and light can not shine clearly through a clouded glass. We need Jesus' help to remove anything that does not reflect him truly.

There was a time when I learned the very truth of the scripture in Phillipians 3:3b "We Christians glory in what Christ Jesus has done for us and realize that we are helpless to save ourselves." As I mentioned before, I had anger and hatred in my heart. I could not remove it however hard I tried.

Finally I put a chair into the middle of the kitchen floor and committed myself to stay there until God removed my anger or somehow removed me from the scene.

My sincerity was tested. I stayed at that chair for a long, long time. But God came through with a miracle I shall never forget. It is as clear in my mind today as it was at that moment.

I've told it before and I'll tell it over and over again!

A breeze came through a window that wasn't on that particular wall. It came through an apple orchard full of blossoms on trees that weren't there. It blew through a hole in my chest that wasn't there and carried away the darkness of self-pity, anger and hate - all those ugly things that were there. The sweet, fragrance brought a peace which has remained all these fifty plus years.

The joy of the moment was beyond expression then and it still is.

Now my greatest joy is to live in Christ, be conscious of him in all things, commune with him always, have my heart open and slanted heavenward. I think that is what the Apostle Paul meant when he said, "Pray without ceasing." It takes practice but it grows more natural through the years.

And the joy of it is "unspeakable and full of glory."

CHAPTER 22
DIE TO LIVE?

Jesus says, "Except a grain of wheat fall into the ground and die, it abides alone. If it dies it will bring forth much fruit." John 12:24

What does this mean to us? It says if we save ourselves we will lose our lives but if we lose ourselves (in Jesus) we will find life and our lives will be very productive.

The cross is the symbol of death. But it is also the symbol of life. There is no resurrection without a cross. We must die to our selfish selves to live in Christ's abundant life.

Jesus died to give us life. We give up our old sinful life to gain the new birth of spiritual life. Baptism is a sign and symbol of this act of burial and resurrection.

The Apostle Paul says, "I am crucified with Christ: nevertheless I live; yet not I, but Christ liveth in me:" (Gal. 2:20a.)

Jesus comes in, in his power and glory, when we yield ourselves up to him. We may not feel it immediately. For most it takes time to become sensitive to the Holy Spirit as he acts within us. The Kingdom of God is Love, Joy, and Peace in the Holy Spirit. The longer we live in the Kingdom of God the more we learn to partake of these spiritual gifts which are the essence of the Kingdom. They become ours when we abandon ourselves to The One Whose They Are, Jesus. This miracle is ours for the earnest, sincere and surrendered asking.

Each higher good is gained through sacrifice—the sacrifice of a lesser good. The lower rung of the ladder must be abandoned to step upon the higher rung. There is no achievement without labor. There is no gain without pain. There is no receiving Christ without giving ourselves.

If you want God's rich blessings in your everyday life, pick up your cross and follow Jesus. He says to you, "My yoke is easy and my burden is light." (Matt. 11:30) Isaiah says, "This is the way. Walk in it." (Isa. 30:21)

CHAPTER 23
CHRIST IN YOU!

That God is in us is an absolute. For he is in all things. The Apostle Paul says, "God was in Christ reconciling the world unto himself." (II Cor. 5:24)

To me that means Jesus is working in and through everything in our world and in our lives to bring us and all mankind into harmony with all the positive things God is. It is God who is the initiator. God is "The Hound of Heaven" as the poet, Thompson, says. He races through the labyrinths of time and experience to catch us when we come to the end of ourselves. As a mother's heart seeks after a child's good so God seeks to bring us to Good. That Good is God, Himself. Love is seeking to bring us to Love.

"The heavens declare the glory of God and the firmament showeth forth his handiwork. Day unto day uttereth speech and night unto night bringeth forth knowledge." (Ps. 19:1&2)

All the universe is telling us GOD IS and "he is a rewarder of them that diligently seek him." (Heb. 11:6b)

All good is in God. If we would have good in our every day living we must invite God, every day, into our minds and hearts.

Dr. Jones says God does not give his gifts without giving himself with them. When we pray and ask God for a "thing," if that thing is good then God is in it. We must accept God in all that we accept from him. We could as soon ask for breath without air as to ask for good without God.

The stamp of Christ is in everything, Jones says. The laws of life and the laws of God are synonymous. The Christ-way is the way life is made to work. Divine law is written into flesh, blood, bone and all things that make up life within and without. When we rebel against God we are, in actuality, rebelling against ourselves. Sin is an act not only against God but also against ourselves. Neither can we act against another without acting against ourselves.

Here is one of Madame Guyon's prayers.

"O, My Lord, Thou wast in my heart, and demanded only a simple turning of my mind inward to make me sense Thy presence. How I was running hither and thither to seek Thee. My life was a burden. I sought Thee where Thou wast not, and did not seek Thee where thou wast indeed. I did not understand the words of Thy Gospel, 'The kingdom of God is within you.'"

When God revealed to her that He was in her and she only needed to look within her own heart she says,

...my heart was changed, ..I experienced God's
presence in my soul. I felt my soul anointed
and healed of all wounds in a moment.
I did not sleep that night because God's love
flowed in me like oil... As time passed, I
seemed different to myself and to others. My
troublesome faults disappeared, being
consumed like debris in a great fire.

In the book, *Heroes of Thought,* (P.24) J. Middleton Murray says. "And if men do not care about the Kingdom [of God] they will find the same lesson taught by life itself. Life cannot be abused. To the judgment seat of God man must take with him only a life that was lived: and the judgment of God and the judgment of life are the same."

That life cannot be abused is a truth sadly revealed in the experiences of many. Perhaps you have witnessed it yourself and known many others who have. Two of our dearest friends were so caught in Satan's trap. I called them and asked if I could tell their story. They gave consent and also sent a note verifying it.

CHAPTER 24
SATAN'S TERRITORY

"The following story is true. It happened in the lives of my husband and me. God sent us a young pastor and his wife to help us hunger after Jesus. Then he sent the Holy Spirit to free us from the power of Satan who had made us his slaves. 'He who the Son sets free is free indeed.' Praise God! Nancy"

Here is Nancy and Rod's story.

Throughout the years Nancy attended church and felt she was a Christian. True, she was a believer. But self, instead of Jesus, was at the center of her life. She actively enjoyed finding fault with others. Talking about people, criticizing them was fascinating activity. In fact, gossiping was her main pleasure.

She didn't realize this spirit was evil. Nor did she know it was growing to consume her.

She was living against life and her way of life was threatening to destroy her and all she had.

At first Sam and I did not know how to handle the angry situation that existed among the people in this church. But earlier, God had shown us our inadequacies, brought us to himself, and prepared us to let him fight our battles. Now God reminded us of the redemptive resources he had given us:

unconditional love and earnest prayer. We set about to use them.

Every morning I arose an hour before the rest of the family and went to the church to pray. There at the altar, I prayed God would show us what to do to bring his peace and love to these people. To become a redemptive body of believers who worshiped together in love and truth was our deepest desire.

My praying at the altar each morning took Nancy's attention. She questioned me about it. I invited her to come pray with me. She rebelled in anger. Later, thinking perhaps it would help her family situation, she agreed to join me. Together we prayed each morning.

Nancy's fine qualities became vivid. She was dependable. I didn't have to wonder if she would be there. She was always on time. She was teachable. When I shared my Jesus-related experiences with her she listened attentively. She became hungry for spiritual things. She began to love the Word of God. In time she added a personal "Daily Quiet Time" to our early morning prayer vigil. She was strong and dedicated, willing to do whatever necessary to reach a goal.

Her husband, Rod became angry at our morning tryst. The more we prayed the angrier he got. Nancy and I learned a bit about persecution from Rod. But she was stalwart in her commitment to learn about Jesus and about living a life surrendered to him.

Satan was using Rod; they were working together to break up our prayer times. The more insulting Rod became the more diligent we were to pray. Other ladies of the church joined us at different times but none were as constant as Nancy and I were.

Rod enlisted his pastor, my husband Sam, to resist Nancy and my joint prayer times. He said it was causing family problems. When Nancy got up early to go pray it disturbed his sleep and affected his work. Sam got after me, telling me to "quit rocking the boat." Their joint efforts became hot, heavy, and relentless. The worse it got the more we depended on God to keep us steady.

Then the miracles began to happen.

At midnight one night I felt called to rise from my bed and pray. There was a certain green, overstuffed chair in the corner of our living room. Often I went there to pray. This night, as I prayed, I sensed an ominous, engulfing darkness. So thick and black was the atmosphere around me that it was stifling. I knew it could only be Satan. I rebuked him in Jesus' name and asked the Holy Spirit to drive him out. For well over an hour I was on my knees striving in the Spirit of intercessory prayer. When peace came, I felt the work God had called me to do was done. I rose and went to bed.

No sooner had I fallen asleep but what a rap came on my bedroom window. "Adele, are you asleep? Get up and let me in."

Sam and I both went out to the living room. Nancy told us the following.

CHAPTER 25
GOD'S POWER

"I was sleeping on my back when I awakened suddenly," Nancy said. "There lying on top of me was a huge snake. His black, shiny, patent leather body was in sections and was as full and long as mine. His beady eyes were directly over mine, close enough to nearly touch my face. In horror I tried to shriek out but no sound came. I tried to turn my head away but I was paralyzed. When I tried to reach over and awaken Rod, I couldn't move. I was petrified with fear and revulsion.

"My hands were lying on the pillow next to my head. I tried to lift my right hand up toward heaven and cry out to God for help. After struggling for a time to no avail, finally, with all my might I was able to lift my hand a couple inches off the pillow. The power of Satan slapped it back down, hard and swift. I couldn't move it again.

"Then I heard God say, 'Look at it. See how full it is? Touch it, see how fat?' I saw that if I tried to poke my finger into it's belly I couldn't make a dent. God said, 'You fed it well. You gave it everything it wanted. Now it has possessed you.'

"Then I remembered how I talked to others about you, Adele. I remembered one time when I had a cake in the oven. I had an unkind thing I wanted to say about you. I could hardly wait for the cake to finish baking. I got dressed; my coat on and purse ready to grab, I was eager to go. As soon as my cake was done, I pulled it out of the oven, turned it out on the cooling racks and was off to do my criticizing and gossiping. I thought of the many mean things I had said and done. Yes, I admitted, I fed the snake well.

"Then the Lord said, 'Now cast it out.'

"That's when I tried to reach my hand up and got it slapped down. I struggled until I was exhausted and I said, 'I can't.'

"Just then out of the periphery of my vision I saw you, Adele, kneeling at my bedside. I knew you were praying for me. You said, 'Go ahead, Nancy, you can do it.' With that I shot my hand up to Jesus and said, 'In Jesus' name you have to go. Go! Go!' And the snake screamed out of my ear like a siren. He slithered his ugly, fat body away from me and six little snakes followed him.

"God named them to me saying, 'Pride, strife, confusion, jealousy, envy, gossip and the biggest one is criticism.'

"After the snakes were gone, the Lord said, 'Now go.'

"I didn't know where he wanted me to go. And I was afraid. But I put my coat over my robe and shivering with fear, I walked to the outside garage. The night was dark and cold and I had no direction. But I backed the car out of the garage and started driving. When I came to your street I thought, Oh sure! I'm supposed to go tell Sam and Adele."

After Nancy told her frightening story we prayed with her and she went home.

What does this experience of Nancy's say to us?

Jesus says we can't serve two masters, God and Satan. We have to choose whom we will serve. Pride, jealousy, envy, strife, anger and unkind intent are all the tools of Satan. Satan is out to destroy us. In giving in to these practices we are assisting Satan with our own spiritual extermination.

Fortunately, Nancy didn't stop there. She went on to use the same dedication to do good that she formerly had to do evil.

This bothered Rod the more. His abuse intensified.

CHAPTER 26
SMALL PERSECUTIONS

God so changed Nancy's life that Rodney was more adamant than ever. He leaned harder on his pastor, my husband Sam, to work with him, saying, "Nancy gets up early to go pray and disturbs my sleep. I work hard all day and I need my rest!"

Sam sympathized with Rod. He didn't like my early rising either. He would gladly have put a stop to it.

Nancy got up at five thirty to dress and drive to the church. We prayed at the altar for an hour. Nancy timed it so she'd get home by seven to make breakfast for Rod before he left for work.

"If those girls are going to pray, why don't they do it during the day when I'm at work?" was one of Rod's many complaints to Sam.

That made sense. Except for the fact that we would not have uninterrupted time during the day when the church was busy with people coming and going. Either one of our homes would not be as busy, still there would be interruptions. But the biggest reason we met at the church in the early morning was that we felt so guided by the Lord. That's the time and place we felt Jesus asked us to meet him.

We went to the church to meet Jesus and to be obedient in

all things.

Another tack Satan and Rod tried was to degrade our prayer time. Rod told Sam he thought we went to the church that early to be alone so we could have improper relationships. Except, he said it in rawer terms.

That was too ridiculous. Sam didn't buy it. But he used it to scare me. It didn't work.

When verbal abuses failed Rod turned to physical abuse. At one time he shoved Nancy against the kitchen cabinets so hard it left bruises.

This kind of abuse worked in the opposite way. We knew Satan was on the run. We prayed all the harder, with earnest, steady faith.

Rod did not leave me out of his verbal abuse and he encouraged Sam to keep on my case. Sam obliged.

One morning at seven o'clock, after our prayer time at the church, one of the dearest old saints of our congregation walked up. He was a short man who had come from Germany. He still carried his German accent and spoke in broken English.

"Brother Varner!" I exclaimed in surprise, "what are you doing here so early?"

"Oh Sister Hooker," he said in a troubled drawl. (At that time our older people called each other "Brother and Sister.")

"I cannot sleep. All night I walk and pray."

"What is troubling you?" I asked.

"God get me up. He say go tell your pastor he take his hands off his wife. She my handmaid. I tell God, 'Bible say lay not your hand on the anointed.' I cannot talk to my pastor. God say, 'Go tell him and tell Rodney, 'Take your hand off your wife, she my handmaid.'"

"How are you going out to Rod's house?" (approximately four miles) I asked.

"I walk."

"There and back is a long way to walk." I reminded him.
He said simply, "I walk."

"You can talk to my husband. You need not fear that. He is
easily entreated. You can feel free in talking to him. He'll hear
you." And I knew Sam would drive Brother Varner out to
Rodney's house in our car.

Sam is a mild-spoken, humble shepherd of the flock. He
loves his people and wants to be all Jesus, the Great Shepherd,
wants him to be. His purpose in reproving me so sharply was
to keep peace in the church. Of course, he didn't know what
Rod was up to. Sam's constant admonition to me was, "Don't
rock the boat. We're making progress. Quit upsetting things!"

I had no desire to upset things. There was an angry spirit in
the church and I wanted to see our church grow in love and
peace. I felt God was calling Nancy and me to prayer so he
could bring the church under the control of the Holy Spirit.
And I wanted to be an obedient child of the Father. That still is
my deepest desire.

"Use me, Oh Lord," was and is my prayer. "Cleanse me of
every sin, within and without, so that this vessel will be fit to
carry the pure water of life."

The Lord works in mysterious ways his wonders to perform.
Sometimes that takes suffering on the part of his servants.

At one time, under the abuse of Rod who gathered forces in
the church, I said, "Lord, do I need to be crucified again?"

Jesus answered me. "No, child. You need die but once."

That was encouraging. I knew I had died on the "kitchen
chair" where I gave my anger, my hate, and my whole self up
to Jesus. He had sent the breath of God to cleanse and fill me.

With that Nancy and I both committed ourselves to be
ridiculed and put down as much as Jesus would allow. After

all, what we were doing was to glorify God. Whatever he needed of us we surrendered to. We were willing. And we went on "suffering for the sake of the cross."

Why do I tell this which is not easy for me to relate?

Because God's children who want to bear fruit may be called on to suffer reproach and rebuff for their testimony. We're not called to be "couch potatoes" in the Kingdom of God. We're called to labor in the fields with Jesus. But if we will plant the seed and cultivate it, God will bless us with an abundant harvest. Thanksgiving and feasting come after the labor of planting, tending and the harvest is gathered in.

Sometimes nothing but deep, earnest, enduring, heartfelt prayer is the answer.

CHAPTER 27
TO KNOW GOD

Nancy and I were in the Word, the Bible. Studying it, memorizing it, striving to conform our lives to Jesus' teaching. In the book of Philippians we came upon the verse where the Apostle Paul says, "That I might know him and the power of his resurrection, and the fellowship of his suffering being made conformable unto his death." Nancy and I took this as our commitment too.

Our whole heart's cry was "Teach me, Oh Master. Conform me to your image that you may use me to the redemption of your people."

Brother Varner had made his statement. But Satan was not defeated.

Rod told Sam he had to get his wife to leave Nancy alone. It was tearing up his marriage. He said, "Nancy isn't the same person any more. It's like living with an angel. Who wants to live with an angel?!" Rod complained bitterly, "I married Nancy and she's gone!"

When Sam told me that my heart shouted, "Praise you, Jesus! Praise you, Jesus!"

Nancy just laughed. She knew she hadn't come that far. We understood our own human weaknesses and often asked the

Lord to save us from them.

Our men were still able to trouble us. But God was still at work in and with us.

Saturdays, at noon, Rod got off work for the weekend. On this particular day Nancy had plans. When Rod came home, lunch was ready. And Nancy was ready; prayed up and surrendered to the Holy Spirit for whatever he had for her to do.

After lunch Nancy said, "Now I want you to take me riding."

Fearing the worst, Rod trembled within. "Where do you want to go?" he asked.

"Just take me," Nancy said. "I'll tell you."

Rod was sure Nancy was going to tell him she wanted a divorce. He knew his hostility toward Nancy was enough to make her want out.

They got into the car.

"Now drive to the park," Nancy said.

The trip to the forty-acre city park with all the hills, lake, trees and flowering shrubs was a short seven miles. They drove in silence.

"Park under this red bud tree," Nancy instructed.

Rod did, with fear and trembling. His biggest fear was about to be realized, he would lose his wife and son. Being an only child, he had no one else. Now Nancy was divorcing him. He would be alone in the world.

Nancy spoke in calm voice.

"I want you to tell me all about your jealousy, anger and meanness."

For over an hour Rod talked, in tears and with rigid jaw. After he finished relating his caustic tale he said, "Now you hate me and you're going to ask me for a divorce."

In agitation he waited for Nancy to say "Yes, I'm leaving

you. I want a divorce."

Instead, in calm, steady voice Nancy said, "No, I'm going to forgive you."

"You're going to do what?!!" Rod shouted. "You're going to forgive me!?" Rod wasn't sure his ears heard what his mind recorded.

"Yes, I'm going to forgive you and love you because Jesus forgave and loved me. We have David. I want us to live the way God wants us to and make a Christian home for him to grow up in."

An exciting time followed with warm, hard hugs, kisses and many, many tears as Rod clung to Nancy.

Then Rod said, "I've got to go to the Hookers. Is it okay if we go now?"

"Take me home and you go. It's yours to do." Nancy said. He did.

CHAPTER 28
CONTRITION

The tires of a car screeched to a halt in front of our house. I was in the kitchen. Sam was in the front bedroom. Without a knock or a "Hello" Rod burst in. He stood in the dinning room and called, "Adele, come here. Sam, come here." There he held out his trembling left hand. His face was soaked with tears that kept running down his cheeks.

"Adele, put your hand in mine," he said.

"Sam, put your hand in mine."

We did.

He cupped his right hand over ours and with quivering lips and halting voice made this proclamation.

"Sam, I've given you a hard time. But I haven't given you near the bad time I've given Adele, here. I want you both to forgive me. I can't fight against that kind of love. As hard as I've worked against you, from this day on I'm going to work for you. That's my promise and you'll see I'm good for my word."

He was.

At the next church business meeting he suggested the pastor's salary was long overdue for a raise. The church agreed and Sam received a substantial salary increase.

That was just one physical evidence of rebirth. But the greater evidence by far was what Rod did after that.

It happened in a Sunday morning church service.

After Sam preached, Rod rose from his seat and walked to the front of the church. "Pastor, I need to say something if that's okay with you."

"You go right ahead, Brother," was Sam's response. *What is he going to do now?* Sam wondered.

Rod turned to the congregation, "I've been a hypocrite among you. I've been one of God's bad boys. I've worked against the pastor. I've been mean to my wife and to the pastor's wife. I've asked the Lord to forgive me and I want you all to forgive me, too. I'm going to kneel at this altar and pray. I know there are those I've influenced. You know who you are. If you want to come up here and pray too, you do it. But I'm confessing my sin to the Lord and asking him to forgive me."

That was a big step toward the great revival that hit our church. For several months no Sunday went by but what people were at the altar praying, seeking God for forgiveness and asking him to use them for his redemptive purposes. For many months baptisms took place every Sunday.

The joy and the glory of God increased in the church. The congregation became a loving, redemptive body of believers. Other churches in the state heard and asked our members to come and share their witness.

We solidified into a precious, peaceful, loving family of God.

CHAPTER 29
JESUS, KEEP US FAITHFUL

"It's required of a steward," the Bible says, "that a man be found faithful." (I Cor. 4:2)

Nancy and I wanted with all our hearts to be faithful so we could be used of God for his glory and the redemption of his children. Faithfully, we continued our tryst with Jesus at the early morning altar. Long before, we had added our own personal quiet time to our altar seeking. Often, in the early part of this time Nancy would call me on the phone shouting with irritation in her voice, "What does this scripture mean?!"

How it amused me! "You've got a hard headed child to work with here, Lord," I said to Jesus. And I'd try to interpret as best I could. Often Jesus helped us so keenly we were utterly amazed. Nancy thought I was smart. I knew better. I knew the Holy Spirit was telling us what Jesus wanted us to hear and learn.

And Rod was good to his word, too.

Together the two of them, Rod and Nancy, became evangels. They visited the sick, prayed for them, carried a burden of intercessory prayer. Many young couples came to them for counsel. Nancy and Rod shared their experiences of arguing and fighting, anger and hate. They openly shared the miraculous redemption of their lives, their marriage and their family.

The Lord blessed Nancy and Rod with many spiritual children. No one in the church worked harder to see souls saved than Rod and Nancy. Together we had many answers to prayer. Others heard about it and came to the church.

To some, God sent us. The first big challenge we had was Marjorie, with terminal cancer. She was sent to her family's hometown hospital to die. In the city hospital we visited her. She lay in a white room, among white sheets, with face and arms as yellow as egg yolk. She was swelled up like a small blimp. In a few days the hospital released her to her husband, saying, "There is nothing more we can do for your wife."

Nancy always had a more courageous faith for healing than I did. She prayed for Marjorie to be healed. I prayed Marjorie would get ready to die. I believed Marjorie would die. Marjorie told us how she hated her mother-in-law and never wanted to see her face. I couldn't think of Marjorie meeting God with a sack of bitterness and hatred on her back. I prayed for her to get ready to meet Jesus.

Day after day we went to see Marjorie, took food for the family, read scripture and prayed. Then, after many, many days, Marjorie surprised us.

She was ready to have her husband bring his mother to visit. Marjorie was going to ask her mother-in-law to forgive her. She did. It wasn't long after that until Marjorie was able to hold food down. Little by little she gained strength. In a few more weeks her husband was able to take her back home to Kansas.

There were many lesser healings in the church family. But in spite of my witnessing these miracles I was plagued with doubt. I was still cutting my teeth in the life of the spirit. I had a long way to go on my path of faith. That was soon revealed to me quite poignantly.

CHAPTER 30
FEAR, SATAN'S TOOL

One night I was sleeping peacefully when I awakened by a voice saying, "Child, come meet me."

It seemed to be coming from the hall at our bedroom door. In curious stillness I listened. Again the voice, clearly audible, called, "Child, come meet me."

I arose and went into the living room to my green, overstuffed "prayer chair." There I began to pray for different ones in the church who were on my heart. That still, small voice within, which I was beginning to recognize, said,

"Go."

Just one word, "Go." But with it came a vision of the big, white, square building which was the city hospital. I knew I was supposed to go there.

I had a timidity which seemed not many people recognized. To go and do something among strangers caused me deep anxiety. To go into the unfamiliar territory of the hospital at midnight greatly intimidated me. But even worse, at that time I was dreadfully afraid of the dark. To go, in the dark, to our unattached garage behind the house was petrifying. I envisioned an evil figure standing at the garage door ready to clap a hand over my mouth and drag me off. And also, to go to a hospital with doctors and nurses wondering why I was there at that hour caused me to tremble with fear, fear, fear!

Formerly, at my wonderful crucifixion, I promised God, for the great gift he gave me, that I would never say "no" to him again.

Though I struggled and begged in prayer for God to let me off, the command stood firm. Just that one word,

"Go."

Fear or no fear, I had to obey. I promised.

Into the bathroom I went, slicked down my hair and quietly sneaked into the bedroom closet for my long coat to cover my long nightgown, which I hiked up and cinched at the waist with a belt. Quietly, oh so quietly, I started to unlatch the front door when my husband stirred. In gruff voice he said, "Where are you going?"

"Out," I answered in timid, kitten-like manner.

"Don't you dare go out of this house. Get back in here and go to bed!"

Although it was gruff it sounded like music to my ears. Hurrah! I've got an excuse not to go to the hospital, I thought.

"See God," I said, "the Bible says, 'Wives obey your husbands.'"

I must admit this was the first time I was so glad and so willing to obey my husband!

But God wasn't letting me off that easy. The same quiet, calm, patient and compassionate inner voice said, "Go or be damned."

Now, I know that sounds harsh and frightful. But it wasn't. It was compassionate. The interpretation was clear. I had a choice. I could not go. But if I didn't, I would be limiting myself. I would be confining myself forever to be functioning on a lesser plain, consigning myself to walk a lower road, crippling myself spiritually to be an untrustworthy child. That was the damnation.

I had committed myself to walk the high road. I had vowed. That meant total obedience without regard to cost.

Here I stood at the cross roads. I hesitated, Do I want to pay the price or sell out?

I unlatched the door and walked out into the dark with fear and trembling. I walked around the house to the garage and car. No dark, evil figure stood there. I drove the whole three blocks to the door of the hospital. Yes, three blocks in daylight was three miles in the dark.

(I praise the Lord, for since then he has delivered me from Satan's irrational fear.)

Shyly I entered the waiting room. There, at midnight, sat five people together on one side of the room! I sat down in a chair on the other side. They were man and wife, ten year old daughter, and a fourteen year old boy, who, I came to know, was a nephew. An older woman, aunt to the wife, sat a few feet from them. What were they doing in the hospital at midnight? I wondered. Then I asked.

The woman, perhaps in her late thirties answered, "My sister is in surgery for a brain tumor at this time."

"Oh, I'm so sorry," I said, "I'll pray for her."

"Thank you, we appreciate that," was the response.

For some moments I sat in silent prayer. Then the lady said, "And what are you here for?"

"—just felt I was supposed to come," I said. "I don't really know why." Then I shared some of the miraculous healings we've had in our family. My mother was instantly healed of a terminal illness. My father, with a weak heart, had surgery without so much as an aspirin. The doctors said it should have killed him.

The husband to the lady spoke up, "Well,¹ we know the biggest miracle of all is the birth of a baby. How can so much wonder and beauty come from so little?" His brief speech put me at ease. I was in friendly territory.

We visited for about an hour when two other people came into the room, the lady's brother and his wife. The man was nice enough looking with a good build. The woman was tall and "decked out" like Jezabel. There was a hardness about her that could not escape one's view.

"The doctor said Jinky's brain is like squeezed out tooth paste," the brother said. "She can't live more than ten minutes."

As I sat there, for me a first and only-time-ever-experience took place. My physical vision seemed to penetrate to the very spirit of the ones in the room. The family sitting, together on the couch, and the aunt were all on one side of the room. The man and woman who came in later stood in the middle of the room about four feet from me. An indescribable hand, more beautiful than pearl, appeared and rested on that woman's shoulder and the voice said, "This is the unbeliever." Then it moved to the man's shoulder and the voice said, "This is the unbelieving one."

"Lord," I said, "what is the difference? An unbeliever or an unbelieving one? I thought they were one and the same."

"Oh no!" the voice said, "This one is simply unbelieving because he is under the sway of the (glamorous) unbeliever."

Right there I learned a lesson about the things of the spirit! "Unbelieving" is not the same as "Unbeliever."

Then the hand pointed to the aunt and the voice said, "This is the religious one." The intonation was one of a cold, stiff, joyless religionist.

Now the hand moved. It unfolded into two hands that went behind the little family on the couch. Here the hands opened, from the thumbs out, and took the shape of wings. They hovered behind the family. The voice said in a most tender, compassionate tone, "And these are the children."

My heart is touched again as I recall the Lord's tenderness.

A warm, caressing spirit was in the hands, as the voice echoed, "These are the children."

Oh how God loves "The Children!!" If we could only, even dimly, perceive how God loves his children, we would be oh so eager and glad to humble ourselves and be "His Children."

There is no spot on earth so treasured by the Father than the heart of his child. This was shown me most poignantly.

Praise You, Jesus, for bringing us to our Loving Father!

CHAPTER 31
DEATH ANGEL

Jinky, this sister who had the brain surgery, did not die in ten minutes as the doctor predicted. She lived on in the hospital for a number of days. I visited her each day. Nancy, I and the other ladies who came to pray with us at the church, prayed for Jinky each morning.

One Sunday afternoon I was alone and again praying at my green, living room "Prayer Chair." A family of young boys in the church were getting pretty wild. I was interceding for them when I heard, "Go. And take the two."

"Take the two?" I questioned, "What two?"

No answer came.

By this time I knew my Lord's voice and I had learned from my mentor, the Holy Spirit, to take one step at a time in strict obedience. It was for me to obey, "Go" and for God to supply "The Two."

I smoothed my hair, put on my coat and stepped out the front door. Just then a car pulled up and parked near our house. It was Nancy and Rod. They were by now fully obedient to God, whatever God directed.

"Hi," I said, "God told me to go to the hospital and pray for

Jinky. And he said, 'Take the two.' I guess that means you. Will you go with me?"

"Sure," Ever-Ready-Nancy said immediately, "There's a young mother we want to see anyway. She was terribly burned in her house fire last night. We want to pray for her."

As we approached the hospital door Nancy said, "You go see Jinky. Rod and I will be in room 101. Come get us when you're ready."

Haltingly and with fear, my feet moved up two flights of stairs and down a long hall as my pounding heart prayed, "Lord, help me! Show me what you want me to do. Help me to pray what you want me to pray!"

A screen was at the door of Jinky's room. I started to walk around it but a kindly, older lady stopped me.

"I've come to see Jinky," I said in half whisper.

"Oh," she whispered back, "Jinky is dying. The doctor asked everyone to leave, even the family. I'm a friend. I'm sitting with her 'till she goes.'"

[Sadly, at that time doctors insisted family members stay away from the dying. Thank the Good Lord that situation has changed!]

"Oh I'm sorry," I said, "I'll pray."

"Thank you," she replied, "please do."

And I backed out of the screened enclosure.

Outside the room, I stood praying. Here I heard the most shocking words ever!

That voice said calmly, "Cast the angel of death out of the room." It was said in such matter-of-fact manner as though I customarily ordered death angels around.

"Cast the angel of death out of the room ?!!" I shouted silently. "I don't know how! I didn't even know death came by angels!"

"Get the two," my mentor said.

Half running, my steps ate up the hall, took the stairs, and flew down another hall to the door of room 101. Seeing me, "The Two" said good bye to their little patient and came.

"What do you want us to do?" Nancy, ever-eager, ever-believing, and ever-courageous asked - as if I should know!

"God said 'Cast the angel of death out of the room.'"

"OK, how do we do it?"

Somehow Nancy always thought I was knowledgeable in these matters. Oh how naive I knew myself to be!

"I don't know." I said, "I didn't even know death came by angels. Let's pray here, then go to the corner there and pray again, then we'll go up to Jinky's door and pray." All those prayers should fortify us for the job, I thought.

Holding hands we prayed at each stop. We were oblivious to whomever might be seeing us. It never dawned on us to care if anyone thought us weird. We were on a mission; a mission of obedience. And, for quivering me, obedience only!

Outside the screen at Jinky's door we stood holding hands and praying. Then I said, "Lord Jesus, in your name we cast the angel of death out of this room. Now in Jesus name, angel of death, you have to go. Death Go! Go!! Go!!!" I said it most emphatically, using the authority of God's commission!

"Now what?" Nancy asked, again as though I would know.

I shrugged my shoulders. "Now we go home. We obeyed. We did what God told us to do. The rest is up to him."

Back to the hospital again I went on Monday. The kind lady was still there. She told me after we prayed Jinky opened her eyes and asked for a cigarette.

When I told this to our missionary ladies, thinking they would rejoice with us, one lady said, "Humph! Why didn't she ask for a cup of water?"

How sad, I thought, She isn't even glad for Jinky's life. She just wants her to be doctrinally correct.

Here's another juncture in the road. Following Jesus we don't get to judge other's behavior. We just get to judge our own. We don't insist people abide by our rules, our religion, our doctrine or position, nor our development. God is both judge and ruler. We don't get to usurp any of his power or his position. That should free us a lot!!

CHAPTER 32
BEAUTIFUL JESUS

Jinky improved enough to go home from the hospital. She gained strength to be up, ride in the car and visit family members in another town.

For several months she made improvement. During this time various of her family members came back to the Lord and to the church they had left because of congregational trouble.

I was happy to visit Jinky in her home. She was bright and alert. But after some time she began to feel sick again. Some weeks later she became bedfast.

One afternoon she called out to her mother, "Oh Mama, come quick!"

Her mother rushed to the bedroom door.

"Look. Oh look Mama! Isn't he beautiful!?" an excited Jinky exclaimed, with eyes focused on a point just beyond the foot of the bed.

"Who, Honey?" her mother asked. "I don't see anyone."

"Oh, of course. You can't see him." Jinky's voice contained understanding but also disappointment.

The next afternoon she called again, "Oh Mama! Come! Look! He's so beautiful!"

This time Jinky's mother understood who Jinky was seeing

and she said, "Yes, Honey. He is beautiful. He is beautiful!" With that Jinky closed her eyes and went into a coma. She stayed in the coma for three days, then expired.

Sam and I were on vacation when Jinky went with Jesus. The morning after we came home I went to visit. Jinky's mother told me about Jinky's last days. "Jesus came to get Jinky himself. But he left her little body here with me for three days to comfort me while I mourned. And I was comforted. A precious peace was given me."

This is just one of the great joys I have been given because of obedience. Do you want to see the Glory of God in your everyday life?

Make yourself available to him in full surrender. Regardless of the cost be submissive and obedient, walk in the face of fear and inhibitions. Say to Jesus in absolute surrender, "Where you lead me I will follow. Where you send me I will go."

And of a truth, you will see the Glory of the Lord in your everyday living.

CHAPTER 33
TEACH ME, OH LORD, MY GOD!

Although the assignment with Jinky was one of the most difficult ever, it was undoubtedly the most wonderful. It was enlightening and oh so rewarding. I learned many good practices from it and yes, many mysteries, too.

One; I learned to walk in the face of fear. Satan can try to control us with fear, greed, lust, unbelief, and all the other tricks he has, but he cannot force them on us. We have the choice to give in to Satan's ploys or to refuse and go God's way in staunch obedience.

Two; I learned Jesus does have the power over life and death. And that prayer can change the course, if it be God's will.

Three; I saw we need not fear death. He sends a friendly spirit to gather us up when our day is done. For some he comes in person. He did both for Jinky. The first time he sent an angel. (I loved it!—after the fact, that is! At the time I was scared nearly out of my skin.) The second time Jesus came for Jinky himself. And as she said, "He is beautiful!"

Four; I learned a little more about the power of two or three gathered in His name. Oh how precious are our brothers and sisters in Christ!

(Please, Jesus, help us cherish each other more.)

Five; I learned that suffering has the "Grace of God" in it. Done with a dependency on Jesus it brings us closer to him and closer to each another. Plus, it is often soul-purifying.

Six; I learned how very much we are spirit and how very little flesh. I was shown the fullness of the spirit of man and I saw that the flesh is a flimsy, temporal shell. [Praise You Lord Jesus!!!! Hallelujah!!]

Seven; I learned that religion is only a path. It has little to do with the purity of the spirit. We can fake religion but we cannot fake the God in us, which is Love and Truth. The path, religion, should lead us to God and not be an end in itself.

Eight; I learned the truth of the Living Word. "..to obey is better than sacrifice and to hearken than the fat of rams." (I Sam. 15:22) There is nothing we can lay on the altar of God with greater worth than a loving, humble, obedient heart.

Nine; I learned our fears, our struggles, our stubbornness cave in when we "walk in the face of them" and go at God's command. God told me to walk in the face of fear and it would dissipate. Sure enough, it did, and my stubborn resistance did too.

Ten; Oh how much I learned of the tender, compassionate, patient, long-suffering love of our Lord, a jewel of unfathomable worth and beauty. He told me I could wear it if I would. All it took was tender compassion; patient, long-suffering, enduring love for others.

Eleven; I learned that one act, like a seed falling into the soil, brings forth a multitude, an abundance of harvest.

God is eager to teach us, his children, if only we are eager to learn. And learning we do with patient persistence, day by day.

CHAPTER 34
JOYOUS HARVEST

Here is the aftermath of this experience with Jinky.

The nephew, Billy, who sat on the couch that midnight when God sent me to the hospital, was the son of the "Unbelieving One." Billy was living with Grandma and Jinky because his step-mother didn't want him with them. Throughout this time I visited with Billy, too. After Jinky left us, Billy came by the house quite regularly to give us a report on the family and on his own activities. He said he, his aunt and family were all going back to church.

Next he told me he gave his heart to the Lord and was attending church regularly. Later he reported that his pastor had asked him to be the church youth leader. On another visit he shared his feelings of being called to the ministry. Then he gave us the thrilling report that he was going to their church college to study for the ministry. The church had given him a scholarship.

After some time the Lord sent us to another church in another state. And we received no further news of Billy. I look back at times and think --- Who knows but what a little courage, very little on my part, and a big lump of obedience (by the grace of God alone) opened the door for a young man to find Jesus and become one of his under shepherds.

Only heaven will count all the souls he touches.

And only heaven can count all the souls Nancy and Rod have gathered into the Kingdom of God. Now after fifty years I know they are still ministering to the troubled, the sick and the needy.

God be praised!

Here is the secret for your everyday living: You cannot—but cannot!—spend time with Jesus, willingly submitting to his will and letting him redeem your nature but what you will have the time of your life!

Joy! Peace! and Love! will walk in your path with you! Believe me. It is true!

(Praise You, Jesus!)

(If by some rare act of God's blessing Billy should read this book, he will recognize the story. How delighted we'd be if he contacted the publisher and got our address. We'd be so happy to hear from him.)

* * * * *

Printed in the United States
821200002B